2ND EDITION

ECONOMICS 101

FROM **CONSUMER BEHAVIOR** TO
COMPETITIVE MARKETS—EVERYTHING
YOU NEED TO KNOW ABOUT **ECONOMICS**

ALFRED MILL with MICHELE CAGAN, CPA

ADAMS MEDIA
NEW YORK   LONDON   TORONTO   SYDNEY   NEW DELHI

Aadamsmedia

Adams Media
An Imprint of Simon & Schuster, LLC
100 Technology Center Drive
Stoughton, Massachusetts 02072

This Adams Media hardcover edition
June 2024
First Adams Media hardcover edition
January 2016

ADAMS MEDIA and colophon are registered
trademarks of Simon & Schuster, LLC.

Simon & Schuster: Celebrating 100 Years of
Publishing in 2024

For information about special discounts
for bulk purchases, please contact Simon &
Schuster Special Sales at 1-866-506-1949 or
business@simonandschuster.com.

The Simon & Schuster Speakers Bureau can
bring authors to your live event. For more
information or to book an event, contact the
Simon & Schuster Speakers Bureau at
1-866-248-3049 or visit our website at
www.simonspeakers.com.

Manufactured in the United States of
America

1 2024

Library of Congress Cataloging-in-
Publication Data
Names: Mill, Alfred, author. |
Cagan, Michele, author.
Title: Economics 101, 2nd edition /
Alfred Mill with Michele Cagan, CPA.
Description: 2nd edition. | Stoughton,
Massachusetts: Adams Media, [2024] |

Series: Adams 101 series | Revised edition of
Economics 101, [2016]
Identifiers: LCCN 2024008176 | ISBN
9781507222386 (hc) | ISBN 9781507222393
(ebook)
Subjects: LCSH: Economics. | BISAC:
BUSINESS & ECONOMICS / Economics /
General | REFERENCE / General
Classification: LCC HB171 .M46126 2024 |
DDC 330--dc23/eng/20240222
LC record available at https://lccn.loc
.gov/2024008176

ISBN 978-1-5072-2238-6
ISBN 978-1-5072-2239-3 (ebook)

Contains material adapted from the
following titles published by Adams Media,
an Imprint of Simon & Schuster, LLC:
Economics 101 by Alfred Mill, copyright
© 2016, ISBN 978-1-4405-9340-6 and
The Everything® Economics Book by David
A. Mayer, copyright © 2010 by Simon &
Schuster, LLC, ISBN 978-1-4405-0602-4.

CONTENTS

INTRODUCTION

If you've ever wanted to understand the basics of the economy, this book is a great first step. From opportunity cost to economic institutions to inflation, understanding economics may appear a daunting task. And our economic theories continue to change: twenty-first-century theories like the New Growth Theory are still being introduced today. However, though things are always changing, your understanding of the principles of economics may keep your financial house in order.

In *Economics 101, 2nd Edition*, you'll have a wealth of updated information that will help you understand economic policy, learn why the financial world works as it does, and keep track of your monetary health. Here, you'll learn helpful information like:

- The imperfections behind the economy with information and behavioral economics
- How COVID-19 impacted supply and demand
- Why modern currencies (like cryptocurrencies) are changing the economic landscape
- The many varying key economic indicators, including ones you may not expect
- How economic institutions (like the World Bank) function

Each informative lesson in the pages of this book brings you closer to economic literacy. Plus, each section shows how real-world situations apply to the lessons they're teaching. For example, you'll learn how Trump tariffs affected international trade, and how COVID-19 brought about a short recession. These ideas will help you make better sense of the economy around you and why people behave as they do in financial matters. This book even broaches topics like the stock market and national debt, making you more aware of financial topics across the board. As you take the time to learn about economics, your life (and perhaps your wallet) will become enriched.

Ultimately, no matter your financial standing, *Economics 101, 2nd Edition* will help you on your quest to learn about economic theory and more. So, let's begin!

WHAT IS ECONOMICS?

Taking the Dismal Out of "The Dismal Science"

You open the door to your fridge and gaze at the food inside and declare, "There's nothing to eat in this house." Later, you walk into a closet full of clothes and then think, "I have nothing to wear." You are faced with scarcity. You never have enough of what you need or want. The fact is, you have plenty to eat and many clothes to wear. You chose to ignore the options you faced then and there, but eventually you know you will relent and eat the apple next to the shriveled grapes at the bottom of the bin, and then put on the shirt and pants you hate. You are a creature of economics. Given scarcity, you look at the choices you face, evaluate, and then choose.

STUDYING SCARCITY

Economics is the study of how individuals, institutions, and society choose to deal with the condition of scarcity. It is fascinating to see how people react to scarcity. Some create complex plans and systems to make sure that everyone gets their fair share of scarce resources. Others make things up as they go along. Everybody practices economics on a daily basis. From a single individual to the largest society on earth, people are constantly engaged in the struggle to survive, make ends meet, and even thrive given the relative scarcity they face.

The people who study these choices are economists. The field of economics is huge because people have an immense range of choices. Some economists study the decision-making of individuals and institutions; others study how nations handle scarcity. Economists develop theories to explain the behavior of whatever it is they are studying. Some of these theories are then tested against real-world data, and sometimes these theories are put into practice without ever being tested. Economists work for universities, financial institutions, major corporations, and governments.

The Child of Philosophy

Economics has been around a long time, though it has not always been known by that name. Philosophers studied scarcity and choice long before the field was so named. The father of modern economics, Adam Smith, was considered a moral philosopher, not an economist.

MICROECONOMICS

The field of microeconomics focuses its attention on the decision-making of individuals and businesses. Microeconomics is primarily concerned with markets for goods, services, and resources. Markets are central to understanding microeconomics. Whenever and wherever buyers and sellers come together to exchange resources, goods, or services, a market is created and the behavior of these markets is of particular interest to economists. Are they functioning efficiently? Do participants have access to adequate information? Who and how many participate in the market? How do the decisions made in one market impact the decisions in a related market?

MACROECONOMICS

Macroeconomics is the study of how entire nations deal with scarcity. Macroeconomists analyze the systems nations create or allow for the allocation of goods and services. The questions they ask are varied and of great interest to individuals and policymakers alike:

- How do you measure the economy?
- Why does unemployment exist?
- How do changes in the amount of money affect the entire economy?
- What impact does government spending or tax policy have on the economy?
- How can you make the economy grow?

SCARCITY

Without scarcity there would be no need for the study of economics. For that matter, if scarcity did not exist, there would be no need for this book. You're not that lucky, however. Scarcity is the universal condition that exists because there is not enough time, money, or stuff to satisfy everyone's needs or wants. The stuff that everyone wants is made from resources.

In an effort to make economics sound more "economic-y," resources are referred to as the factors of production. The factors of production include land, labor, capital, and entrepreneurship.

- Land is inclusive of all natural resources and not just some random piece of property. Trees, mineral deposits, fish in the ocean, groundwater, and plain old land are all included. Land can be divided into renewable and nonrenewable natural resources.

Renewable resources, like pine trees and farmed chickens, are easily replenished. Nonrenewable resources, like oil reserves and Atlantic cod, are difficult to replenish. The payment for land and the resources it contains is referred to as rent.

- Labor refers to people with their skills and abilities. Labor is divided into unskilled, skilled, and professional. Unskilled labor refers to people without formal training who are paid wages to do repetitive tasks like make hamburgers or perform assembly-line production. Skilled labor refers to people who are paid wages for what they know and what they can do. Welders, electricians, plumbers, mechanics, and carpenters are examples of skilled laborers. Professional laborers are paid wages for what they know. Doctors, lawyers, engineers, scientists, and teachers are included in this category.

- Capital in economics does not refer to money, but to all of the tools, factories, and equipment used in the production process. Capital is the product of investment. Stop. Isn't that confusing? Up until now you have probably lived a happy life thinking that capital was money and that investing is what you do in the stock market. Well, sorry. Capital is physical stuff used to make other stuff, and investment is the money spent on buying that stuff. To make capital, you have to have capital. Because capital is always purchased with borrowed money, it incurs an interest payment.

Money Talks

allocation

Economists describe getting the right resources to the right people as allocation. Allocative efficiency occurs when marginal benefit (the maximum a consumer is willing to pay for something) equals marginal cost (the cost to manufacture one unit). When this condition is met, the greatest benefit accrues to society.

TRADE-OFFS AND OPPORTUNITY COST

Making an Assumption Out of You and Me

Whenever you use a factor of production, a cost is going to be incurred. Why? The factors of production are limited, not limitless. As a result, whenever you choose to use land, labor, capital, or entrepreneurship for one purpose, you lose the ability to use it for another. Take a resource like labor—your labor. Say that you can spend an hour writing a book, teaching a class, or weaving a hammock. The choices you face are called trade-offs. Assume you choose to weave a hammock. You can neither teach a class nor write a book in that hour of time. If writing a book is your next best alternative, then economists would say that the opportunity cost of spending an hour weaving a hammock is the hour you could have spent writing a book. Opportunity cost is the next best alternative use of a resource.

Implicit and Explicit Costs

Opportunity cost is sometimes referred to as implicit cost. For any productive activity there are explicit costs like labor, raw materials, and overhead, which are easily calculated, and there are the implicit costs, which are more difficult to assess.

CONSIDERING OPPORTUNITY COST

Suppose it's a beautiful Friday morning and you think to yourself, "I could go to work like I'm supposed to, I could stay home and sleep away the day, or I could fly to Cozumel and hang out on the beach and do some scuba diving." Assume that you chose to take the trip to Cozumel, but going to work was your next best alternative. What was the cost of your trip? You paid for the taxi to the airport, the plane ticket, an all-inclusive hotel package, and a dive on Palancar Reef. Was that your only cost? No. You also sacrificed the money you could have made working. Opportunity cost is a bummer. Make sure to always count it when making a decision.

MARGINAL ANALYSIS

Economists like to think of people as little computers who always count the benefit of their decisions versus the cost of those decisions. Because you usually make decisions one at a time, economists refer to the benefit of a decision as marginal benefit. Marginal benefit can be measured in dollars or utils, whichever you prefer. Utils are the amount of utility or happiness you get from doing something. They can be converted into dollars easily.

Say that you like to swim laps in the pool for an hour. How many utils do you receive from swimming laps? How much would you have to be paid to not swim laps? If your friend were to keep offering you ever-increasing amounts of money to not swim in the pool, then it is probably safe to assume that the dollar amount you accept to not swim in the pool is at least equal to the amount of happiness or utility you would have received had you taken a swim. If it takes $20 to keep you from swimming, then you value swimming no more than $20. Swimming is worth 20 utils to you.

Marginal cost is a related concept. Marginal cost is simply what it costs to either produce or consume one extra unit of whatever it is you are producing or consuming. Go back to the swimming example. Assume that swimming in the pool has a marginal cost of $5. If you earn 20 utils from swimming, would you pay $5 to earn $20 worth of benefit? Of course you would. Now assume that swimming in the pool costs $20.01. Would you spend $20.01 to earn $20 worth of benefit? Probably not. Economists conclude that you will swim as long as the marginal benefit exceeds or equals the marginal cost. For you that means you will swim as long as the marginal cost is less than or equal to $20. If the marginal benefit outweighs the marginal cost, you'll probably do it. If the marginal benefit is less than the marginal cost, you probably would not do it. If the marginal benefit equals the marginal cost, it means you are indifferent.

ASSUMPTIONS IN ECONOMICS

Economists make certain assumptions when they're talking about their favorite subject. They expect you to know (and agree with) these assumptions. The three big ones are:

1. **Nothing else changes.** Whenever economists make an argument such as "If income taxes fall, then consumption increases," it should be understood as: "If income taxes fall *and nothing else changes*, then consumption increases." Did you catch the difference between the two statements? *And nothing else changes* is also referred to as the ceteris paribus assumption.

Loosely translated, ceteris paribus means "to hold all other things constant." So as you continue reading this book, remember that all statements about cause-and-effect relationships are made with the ceteris paribus assumption.

2. **People are rational and behave rationally.** Another assumption made by economists, and a big one at that, is that people behave rationally. Economists assume that people's choices are made with all available information taken into account as well as the costs and benefits of the choice. Furthermore, economists assume that the choices make sense. The assumption that people behave rationally is subject to debate among different schools of economic thought, but for most economic decisions it is a useful assumption.

3. **People are selfish.** The last assumption made by economists is that people are self-interested. First and foremost, people think of themselves whenever the time arrives to make a decision. Pure altruism is not possible in economics. Economists cynically assume that human behavior is motivated by self-interest. For example, a grenade is thrown into a trench with a platoon of soldiers and one soldier sacrifices his life by jumping on top of the grenade, thus saving the others. To economists, this soldier instantly calculated the marginal benefit and marginal cost of the decision, determined that the marginal benefit of saving his fellow soldiers outweighed the marginal cost of his life, and jumped on the grenade as an act of utility, maximizing self-interest. He saved his friends in order to maximize *his* utility as a soldier. From a purely economic perspective, the benefit of saving his platoon was more than the cost of his life.

The assumptions economists make are subject to criticism and debate. Many critics believe that the field tends to be too abstract and theoretical to have any real-world value. Most economists predicted a recession in 2023 that never occurred, which seems to support the view that economics ignores human psychology at its own peril.

Economics is at a turning point as a field of study, and the assumptions that economists hold dear need to be carefully examined. Instead of being tidy, abstract, and mathematical like physics, economics must become a little more messy, complex, and organic, like biology.

Money Talks

consumption
Household spending on new domestic goods and services.

THE EMERGENCE OF FREE TRADE AND THE IMPORTANCE OF COMPARATIVE ADVANTAGE

Why All Roads Lead to Rome

Which leads to a higher standard of living, dependence on others or complete self-sufficiency? Before you answer the question, consider which approach better represents your life. Do you have a job and pay all your own bills, or do you live at home with your parents while they foot the bill for your upkeep? If you are on your own, you most likely consider yourself to be self-sufficient. If you are still living at home with your parents, you probably consider yourself to be somewhat dependent. The truth, however, is whether you are on your own or living at home, you are highly dependent on others for the food you eat, the clothes you wear, and the roof over your head. In order for you to get what you need and want and enjoy a higher standard of living, you must trade with others.

The History of Trade in Sixty Seconds

From the beginning of human existence, trade was a simple matter. For example, families exchanged food with their neighbors. Over time, trade expanded as people were exposed to new, desirable goods from faraway places. As tribes evolved into empires, trade grew in importance. This growth in trade led to the emergence of the influential merchant class. These merchants braved hardships in search of profit, and their activities helped to form the modern world. Although the scale of trade has grown incredibly throughout history, what has not changed is that trade always occurs between individuals.

MERCANTILISM

One early theory of trade was mercantilism, which dominated seventeenth- and eighteenth-century European trade policy. Mercantilism is founded on the idea that a country, and therefore individuals, is better off if the value of a country's exports is greater than the value of its imports. Under mercantilism, the more gold a country amassed, the wealthier it became. As a result, countries competed to import cheap natural resources and then convert them into more expensive manufactured goods for export. It is easy to see why the countries of Europe were eager to compete against each other in order to colonize and exploit the newly discovered and resource-rich Americas.

Mercantilism had an obvious flaw. If a country is always trying to export more than it imports and everyone else is playing the same game, then someone is going to lose. In order to maintain a country's export advantage, governments enacted many laws and taxes that distorted the flow of goods without necessarily making the people better off. In the end, mercantilism created a win-lose condition that harmed more than it helped.

FREE TRADE

The insights of eighteenth-century Scottish thinker Adam Smith were influential in bringing an end to mercantilism. He and others at the time saw governments' mercantilist policies as misguided and prone to influence by special interests. He argued in *The Wealth of Nations* that if a country specialized in what it produced best and freely traded those products, then society would be better off. Adam Smith saw wealth as being the sum total of all that the people of a nation produced. In his view, free trade led to greater wealth, even if it meant that sometimes you imported manufactured goods from people in other countries.

One argument used in support of the idea of free trade is the theory of comparative advantage. Whereas Adam Smith had argued for a country to specialize in what it does best and then trade with others, another influential thinker, David Ricardo, argued that it is better for a country to specialize in what it produces at the lowest opportunity cost, and then trade for whatever else it needs. These two concepts are referred to as absolute advantage and comparative advantage.

Absolute Advantage

An absolute advantage exists if you can produce more of a good or service than someone else, or if you can produce that good or service faster than someone else. An absolute advantage implies that you are more efficient—that is, able to produce more with the same number of resources. For example, Art can write one hit song per hour, whereas Paul can write two hit songs per hour. Thus, Paul has an absolute advantage in songwriting.

Comparative Advantage

A comparative advantage exists if you can produce a good at a lower opportunity cost than someone else. In other words, if you sacrifice less of one good or service to produce another good or service, then you have a comparative advantage. In the example given earlier, Art and Paul are songwriters, but what if both are also capable of performing complex brain surgery? If Art and Paul can both successfully complete two brain surgeries in an hour, then which has a comparative advantage in songwriting, and which has a comparative advantage in brain surgery?

To calculate the comparative advantage, you must determine the opportunity cost that each person faces when producing. In Art's case, for every hit song he writes, he sacrifices two successful brain surgeries. In an hour, Paul can produce either two hit songs or two brain surgeries. This means that Paul sacrifices one brain surgery for every hit song he writes, and therefore, has the comparative advantage in songwriting. Art, on the other hand, has the comparative advantage in brain surgery, because for every brain surgery he performs, he only sacrifices half of a hit song, compared to Paul, who sacrifices a whole hit song for the same surgery. In conclusion, Art should specialize in brain surgery and Paul in songwriting because that is where they find their comparative advantage.

Efficiency and Comparative Advantage

It is easy to overlook comparative advantage when determining who should produce what. Just because one person might be more efficient than another does not always mean that that person should be the one doing the task. Remember to always count the opportunity cost.

COMPARATIVE ADVANTAGE AND ECONOMIC CHANGE

The theory of comparative advantage allows you to better understand how the American economy has changed over the last sixty years. In that time period, the United States transitioned from a low-skilled, manufacturing economy to a high-skilled, diversified economy. Sixty years ago, most of your clothes would have been produced domestically, but today the tags on your clothing indicate that they were manufactured in places as diverse as Vietnam, Bangladesh, Indonesia, Thailand, and China.

In the same time period, a great wave of technological innovation and other cultural advances have taken place. For example, if you were to poll a group of high school freshmen about their post–high school plans sixty years ago and another group today, you would likely discover that today's students are far more likely to pursue higher education than they were in the 1940s and 1950s. In the past, dropping out of high school and working at the mill or the factory was the norm; today, dropping out of high school is cause for concern. There are more jobs as well as more job titles than there were sixty years ago. In other words, there are greater opportunities today than there were sixty years ago. Of course, this comes with one major catch: You must have the education or training in order to take advantage of the opportunity.

So what does this have to do with comparative advantage? An example might help. Consider 100 typical American high school students and then consider 100 young people of the same age in Bangladesh. In which country is the opportunity cost of producing a T-shirt higher? If you look at the American students, you may determine that they have more opportunities than the Bangladeshi. When Americans specialize in T-shirts, more potential doctors, nurses, teachers, engineers, mechanics, business managers, machinists, and social workers are sacrificed than in Bangladesh, where the majority of workers will most likely become subsistence farmers. The opportunity cost of producing T-shirts is much lower in Bangladesh than in America, and therefore Bangladesh has a comparative advantage in producing T-shirts. Even though the United States has the capacity to produce T-shirts more efficiently (absolute advantage), from an economic standpoint, it makes sense to trade pharmaceuticals, refined chemicals, capital equipment, and know-how for T-shirts.

INTERNATIONAL TRADE AND TRADE BARRIERS

Free Trade Without Borders

When trade is both voluntary and free, the buyer and the seller both benefit (if you buy a quart of milk, the dairy farmer gets money and you get milk without having to milk a cow). Because voluntary free trade is mutually beneficial, it creates wealth. Wealth is nothing more than the collective value of all you own. In an interesting experiment from the Foundation for Teaching Economics, a group of participants were each given a random object to which they assigned a value. Then the group traded their objects freely. Soon after, participants were again asked to assign a value to the object in their possession. The sum of the second set of values was greater than the first. Without anything new being added, wealth was (and is) created through the simple act of voluntary free trade.

INTERNATIONAL TRADE

When you trade with people in other countries, the same results of mutual benefit and wealth creation occur. Prior to World War II, trade agreements between nations were for the most part bilateral—that is, between the two parties—with special interests protected and trade barriers (such as taxes on imports and exports) common. The benefits of free trade were not realized, and nations drifted toward isolationism and protectionism.

Toward the end of World War II, representatives from much of the industrialized free world gathered in Bretton Woods, New Hampshire, to address the economic issues that were often the cause of international conflict. The conference produced the International Monetary Fund (IMF) and the World Bank, but not a trade organization for encouraging international cooperation. In 1947, many nations including the United States came together and formed the General Agreement on Tariffs and Trade (GATT). The goal of GATT was to reduce trade barriers so that member countries could equally enjoy the benefits of free trade.

The growth in international trade was accompanied by a rise in living standards among the members of the agreement. In 1995, the GATT became the World Trade Organization (WTO). Under GATT and later the WTO, more and more countries have become supporters of fewer barriers to trade. As a result, international trade has continued to expand, and many nations have reaped the benefits. For example, since joining the European Union (EU) and opening itself to international trade, Ireland has gone from being one of Europe's poorest countries to one of its wealthiest.

THE CASE AGAINST INTERNATIONAL TRADE

Despite its obvious benefits, free international trade has many detractors:

- Environmentalists are concerned that as countries specialize, production will concentrate in countries that have fewer regulations to protect the environment from pollution and habitat destruction.

- Labor unions oppose free trade on the grounds that production will shift toward low-wage countries that have little or no union representation, and therefore negatively impact their membership.
- Human rights activists often oppose free trade as production shifts toward countries where working conditions are miserable and often inhumane, and where workers are not afforded the same rights and privileges as in industrialized nations.
- Politicians and their constituents concerned with loss of national sovereignty often oppose free trade agreements on the grounds that decisions affecting the nation are being made by an international body not directly subject to the people.

A LOOK AT TRADE BARRIERS

From time to time, countries will seek to tax, limit, or even ban international trade. Why? Even though voluntary trade is mutually beneficial, the benefits are spread out over society, and the costs are sometimes borne directly by a specific group. People might have a strong interest in preserving their industry, raising tax revenue, saving the environment, or even creating social change. At times a country might limit trade in order to punish another country. Tariffs, quotas, and embargoes are a few of the tools that a country will use in order to accomplish these other interests.

Tariffs

A tariff is a tax on trade. Tariffs can be used to raise revenue for the government or to benefit a certain segment of the economy. For example, the Trump administration imposed several tariffs in 2018, including tariffs on washing machines, solar panels, and hundreds of Chinese goods. The stated goal was to decrease imports and boost American manufacturing and jobs, but that didn't pan out as expected. The solar panel industry lost approximately 62,000 current and future jobs, according to the Solar Energy Industries Association (SEIA). The tariffs also placed a burden on American businesses that imported parts, resulting in reduced US manufacturing. At the same time, those tariffs resulted in nearly $80 billion of additional tax revenue in 2018 and 2019. As of September 2023, the Biden administration has kept many of the unexpired tariffs in place.

Tariffs are not without their downsides:

- Protective tariffs can impose additional taxes on small businesses and consumers, driving up prices and limiting purchasing power.
- Revenue tariffs often fail to raise tax revenue because people stop buying the now-expensive imports.
- Export tariffs might give producers an incentive not to produce.

Quotas

Quotas are limits on trade. Instead of a tax on imports, you might use a quota to limit the number of imported goods coming into your country. In the 1970s and 1980s, US automobile manufacturers and labor unions supported government quotas on foreign car imports to limit competition and preserve American jobs. The result was higher prices and lower quality.

Money Talks

price

The monetary amount for which consumers and producers buy and sell some quantity of a good or service.

Eventually, Japanese and German firms bypassed the quotas by establishing their factories in the United States. In the end, domestic producers faced more competition at home, and labor unions suffered as foreign firms established their factories in states where unions had less power.

Quotas create other problems as well:

- They do not generate tax revenue for the government, but do create more responsibility.
- They provide an incentive to smuggle goods illegally due to the limitations they place on imported goods, thus creating black markets.
- They may be manipulated by foreign firms to limit competition from other foreign firms. For example, if there is a quota on German cars imported into the United States, then the German firm that first fills the quota has effectively blocked other German firms from competing in the American market.

Embargoes

An embargo is a ban on trade with another country. The purpose of an embargo is usually to punish a country for some offense. The US currently imposes trade embargoes against countries including Cuba, North Korea, Syria, and Iran. Once again, you might consider who benefits from the trade embargo in order to understand why it is still in place.

TRADITIONAL, COMMAND, AND MARKET ECONOMIES

That's Not the Way We Do Things!

Why are some countries so rich and others so poor? Does the presence of abundant natural resources account for a country's wealth? Why is there such a lack of economic development among different Indigenous groups around the world? How important is government to an economy and what are the government's appropriate economic roles? A study of different economic systems will shed some light.

DIFFERENT ECONOMIC SYSTEMS

In order to survive, societies must make decisions about how to best use their scarce resources (land, labor, capital, and entrepreneurial ability). Economists have concluded that for societies to survive with their limited resources, they must answer three basic questions:

1. What to produce?
2. How to produce?
3. For whom to produce?

Throughout history, people have developed a variety of systems to answer these questions. Most primitive societies developed what economists refer to as traditional economies. With the development of civilization came command economies, and following the Enlightenment, market economies finally emerged. In addition, combinations of these primary systems developed, including communism, socialism, and capitalism (discussed later in the book).

The Other Reason to Remember 1776

The eighteenth century, also known as the Age of Reason, or the Enlightenment, saw a fundamental shift in the way people viewed their world. The year 1776 was especially important, for it not only was the year that Thomas Jefferson wrote the Declaration of Independence, but it was also the year that Adam Smith published *The Wealth of Nations*.

Traditional Economies

In a traditional economic system, the questions of what and how to produce for whom are answered by tradition. If you've seen a documentary on a primitive culture, then you've also seen a traditional economy in action. The Kalahari's San people live in one of the world's harshest environments, where even the most basic resources are in meager supply. In order to survive and have enough food, the San have developed a division of labor based on gender. Women perform the food gathering and men perform the hunting. The food is then shared with the whole tribe. In this type of system, stability and continuity are favored over innovation and change. The roles of the people are defined by gender and status in the community. In this system, the old, young, weak, and disabled are cared for by the group. The group shares the few possessions they have, and private property is an alien concept. For the most part, everyone in this system understands his or her relationship to the community, and as a result, life hums along in a fairly predictable way.

Command Economies

As hunter-gatherer societies grew and eventually exhausted their natural food supplies, some survived by becoming sedentary farmers. With the advent of farming came a need for an organized system of planting, harvesting, and storing crops. This required a greater amount of structure compared to a traditional economy. In order to ensure the survival of the society, decisions had to be made about what crops to grow and how much of the harvest to store. Over time, decision-making became centralized, and the command economic system developed. The key characteristic of the command economy is centralized decision-making. One leader (or a group of powerful individuals) makes the key economic decisions for the entire society.

At Your Command

During World War II, the United States practiced command economy when the government took over factories and planned production for the war effort. Every aspect of American life was in some way influenced by government involvement in the economy. Even today you can see the influence. The modern payroll withholding system was instituted during the war to provide the government with a steady stream of tax revenue.

Examples of command systems include most, if not all, ancient civilizations, plus the communist countries of today. The pharaohs of Egypt represent the centralized decision-making present in a command economy. The pharaoh and their various officials made the key economic decisions of what to produce, how to produce, and for whom to produce. The decisions might have gone something like this: "I command you to construct a big pyramid of brick and mortar using slaves for labor, and all of it is for me." The advantage of this type of system is the ability for decision-makers to produce rapid changes in their society. For example, Soviet dictator Joseph Stalin's five-year plans quickly transformed the Soviet Union from a peasant based agrarian society into one of the world's industrial superpowers.

History reveals the tragic downside of command economic systems. As previously discussed, the pharaohs used enslaved laborers, and Stalin's five-year plans were only accomplished through the forced relocation of millions of people and at the cost of millions of lives. Rarely do the decision-makers meet the wants and needs of the common citizen. The citizens serve the economy and state as opposed to the economy and state serving the citizens. North Korea is a perfect example. Property belongs only to the state. Many workers have little personal incentive to produce, and those that do may have little regard for quality. Individuality, innovation, and variety are completely lacking in the command system.

Market Economies

In total contrast to the command economic system is the market economy. Market economies are characterized by a complete lack of centralized decision-making. As opposed to top-down planning, market economies operate bottom-up. Individuals trying to satisfy their own self-interest answer the questions of what, how, and for whom to produce. Private citizens, acting on their own free will as buyers or sellers, trade their resources or finished products in the market in order to increase their own well-being. Though it might appear counterintuitive, market economies achieve greater abundance, variety, and satisfaction than either traditional or command economic systems.

Although they cannot be classified as pure market systems, Hong Kong, the United States, Australia, and New Zealand are representative of market economies. In each you will see a greater variety of goods and services being produced than anywhere else. Also, because the focus is not on serving the state, individuals are free to choose their vocation, own private property, and determine for themselves how to best use the resources they possess. Markets reward innovation, productivity, and efficiency but discourage complacency, idleness, and waste. If markets have a downside, it is that those who are unable or unwilling to produce because of either circumstance or choice are often sidelined and unable to enjoy the benefits of the system.

Money Talks

productivity
The amount of output produced with a given number of resources.

MODERN ECONOMIC THEORIES

This Isn't Your Parents' Economics

Today's economic theories look at the traditionalists in compelling new ways as our society and economy change. They take challenges like CEO vs. worker pay, the exorbitant costs of child care, and the ways people behave in real life into account, rather than just consulting the same old economic models. Psychology and behavior play key roles in these new ideas, which better reflect how people's thoughts and emotions influence their economic actions (like what, when, and how much they buy).

THE MINSKY MOMENT

In his 1975 paper "The Financial Instability Hypothesis," American economist Hyman Minsky identified the triggers signaling sudden economic collapse, such as when bubbles burst or markets tumble abruptly after a long stretch of bullish sentiment. Stability breeds instability was his mantra: When the economy is stable, it will probably become unstable very soon. This predictive premise all hinges on debt accumulation.

His main theory, the Financial Instability Hypothesis, defines what leads up to a sudden economic fall, shining a light on past economic difficulties and predicting probable future problems. This hypothesis gave birth to the famous Minsky Moment, which describes that abrupt shift from stability to instability, based on changes in lending and borrowing behavior. According to Minsky, there are three stages of credit lending that predict what will happen next:

- Hedge
- Speculative borrowing
- Ponzi

Minsky believed that the system is designed to suffer periodic shocks in predictable cycles that will lead to bubbles bursting and economic fallout.

Hedge

The hedge phase occurs when the market is recovering from a market collapse and beginning to restabilize. People and institutions remain financially cautious and risk averse. Tight credit policies limit lending to the highest quality borrowers, who borrow only as much as they can easily afford to repay.

Speculative Borrowing

As business profits, stock market indicators, and the general economy improve, lenders become lax with their guidelines. Additionally, borrowers ask for as much money as they can get. Payments are often just beyond the comfort zone of borrowers, though they can still meet at least the interest portion comfortably.

Ponzi

This is the final phase before the downfall. Continued economic optimism leads to riskier decisions, powered by "irrational exuberance," a feeling that things are good and will stay that way. Asset values—like home prices and stocks—keep growing. People and businesses take on more and more debt, along with higher levels of risk. Borrowers feel the strain of making their payments and often have difficulty meeting their obligations, leading potentially to economic collapse, burst bubbles, and recession.

NEW GROWTH THEORY

New Growth Theory encompasses many new ideas and takes a fresh perspective on what drives economic growth: people. Unlike traditional and neoclassical (updated versions of older work) economic theories that focus on supply and demand, production costs, and diminishing returns, New Growth Theory (NGT) posits that people's wants and needs are the key drivers of prosperity. A key founder of this theory, Paul Romer, highlighted his endogenous growth theory in the late 1980s and early 1990s. The NGT basically states that per-person gross domestic product (GDP) will always grow because people continually pursue more wants, needs, and profits.

NGT emphasizes four core ways that people actively impact the economy:

1. **Knowledge:** People access all the information they need to make informed decisions that will affect the economy.
2. **Technology:** People innovatively use and create technology to gain greater access to the economy and generate profits.
3. **Entrepreneurship:** People pursue their personal and financial desires by investing and generating money that allows them to meet their needs.
4. **Innovation:** People continually invent new products and processes, increasing competition and maximizing profitability.

Human Capital

NGT highly values human capital, considering it any economy's most valuable asset. Human capital encompasses the knowledge and skills that workers of every level bring to the table. According to NGT, governments should support new ideas and innovations to further economic growth. They can do this by providing access to better education and by encouraging research and development in the private sector.

Knowledge Is a Limitless Resource

You've heard that "knowledge is power," and it is. But it's also a key resource, a form of economic capital. In NGT, knowledge capital is an important aspect driving innovation and technology. People can control how much knowledge they have—their personal knowledge capital bank—by choosing to try to learn new things, and by putting effort into their studies. Those choices are powered by profit motive, or how much their knowledge capital can return in economic terms.

PROSPECT THEORY

"Prospect Theory," published in 1979 by Daniel Kahneman and Amos Tversky, examines and explains how investors make choices, taking emotional reactions into account. Earlier economic theories ignore this key aspect of behavioral economics. Prospect Theory brings it to the forefront.

One key premise is loss aversion; this is when people are given equal choices, but one of those is expressed in terms of loss, so they'll choose the other option. For example, if a person is offered a choice between getting $50, or getting $100 if they agree to give $50 of that to charity, people will choose the straight $50. Even though the outcome of getting $50 is the same, people will avoid the choice with loss involved.

Another is certainty bias, where people prefer certain outcomes as opposed to probable outcomes, even when both theoretically lead to the same conclusion. For example, given a choice between a definite $100 or a fifty-fifty chance of winning $200, most people would opt for the $100. It's like the "bird in the hand" adage of economic theory.

In Prospect Theory, presentation of the options plays an outsized role in the final choice. In a larger economic sense, businesses and advertisers can use this bias to steer people toward desired choices.

Prospect Theory in Two Phases

According to Prospect Theory, people go through two phases when making decisions: editing and evaluation. During the editing phase, they assess and prioritize information, narrowing down which pieces they'll use in the decision process. They decide what's important and ignore what's not. But during this process, biases like loss aversion can affect which information makes the cut. That can lead to poorer decision-making, which is irrational in the economic sense.

In the evaluation phase, people make those decisions based on the information from the editing phase. They link probabilities to their options, weighing the odds and appeal of each potential outcome. While this seems rational, risk aversion and inherent biases can lead to suboptimal choices. People tend to lean toward options that minimize perceived loss potential instead of maximizing possible gains.

Overcoming Bias to Make Rational Choices

With knowledge of Prospect Theory and their own biases, people can refocus their options to make more rational decisions. For example, instead of looking at outcomes as potential gains or losses, they could simply compare the value of each choice. Similarly, they can purposely include low-probability outcomes during the editing phase to overcome certainty bias. By reframing choices with an eye toward bias, individuals can make better economic decisions.

Money Talks

risk aversion

The tendency of an individual to have a low risk tolerance and avoid risky options, even when those options are expected to have better outcomes.

INFORMATION AND BEHAVIORAL ECONOMICS

The New Schools

Classical economic theories base a lot of their assumptions on perfection. They assume everyone has access to the same perfect information, for example, and that people behave in perfectly rational ways. Modern economic theories turn those ideas upside down and consider all the imperfections that drive the economy. Two new schools born out of that new thinking include information economics and behavioral economics, and these theories have changed our understanding of what's really behind economic activity and growth.

INFORMATION ECONOMICS

Our world runs on information. It drives decision-making about everything, from which cereal to buy to which candidate to hire to which stocks to include in a portfolio. Information economics explains how differences in information affect the overall economy.

Joseph Stiglitz was a key player in the development of information economics, and his theories on information asymmetry earned him a Nobel Prize. This idea basically states that information is always imbalanced, or asymmetrical, between any two actors in the market—one of the parties may have more information than the other.

Asymmetric Information

While it might seem at first like asymmetric information is a bad thing, it actually helps the economy in a lot of ways. For example, many people specialize in particular areas of information, like doctors, economists, and stunt drivers. This allows for a wider variety of professions and professional knowledge, which benefits the economy and society as well.

On the downside, asymmetric information can also be costly to the economy overall. For example, limited or selective information can lead to market failures and other economic consequences. Asymmetric information can also give rise to fraud that leads to increasing costs in the economy as a whole. For example, people hiding information when applying for health insurance leads to higher-than-expected costs for insurance companies, and that in turn leads to higher premiums overall.

The Lemon Problem

Back in 1970, George Akerlof published his "lemon" theory, which is based on asymmetric information and the used car market. The main idea states that the used car market is full of sellers who know more about the real value of their vehicles than any potential buyers. It makes buyers wary of paying more than an average value, even for a car that's in truly better-than-average condition. This economic behavior favors the seller when the car is a lemon, meaning it has a significant defect, but puts them at a disadvantage with a premium vehicle.

The theory applies to the economy well beyond the used car market. It's especially illuminating when looking at financial markets, which include things like investments, insurance, and credit.

Borrowers, for example, know more about their financial situations than potential lenders do.

Knowing in advance that this asymmetry can cause pricing problems leads the parties to figure out ways to overcome them. For example, a used car seller can offer warranties, protecting buyers from the consequences of buying lemons.

Take My Wife...

George Akerlof is famous for his Nobel Prize win, his renowned paper "The Market for Lemons: Quality Uncertainty and the Market Mechanism," and his work as a professor at Berkeley. But he's most well known for being married to Janet Yellen, former chair of the US Federal Reserve.

BEHAVIORAL ECONOMICS

Traditional economic views tend to leave out a big piece of the puzzle: psychology. When you add that back in, you get behavioral economics, a type of economics that attempts to understand why people make seemingly irrational decisions by using examples of human behavior. A perfectly rational decision weighs the costs and benefits of options. But people don't work that way; our choices are guided by emotions, biases, framing, and dozens of other psychological factors. That leads to irrational choices, at least in the economic sense.

The Behavioral Economists

This branch of economics has intrigued many economists, leading to several Nobel prize winners including:

- **Herbert Simon (1978),** known for his theory on bounded rationality that states that people use reasoning shortcuts to come up with "good enough" decisions instead of the best possible ones
- **Gary Becker (1992),** known for his work on the motives behind decision-making and consumer mistakes
- **Richard Thaler (2017),** known for his theory on nudging people into making decisions (also called choice architecture) by steering them in a particular direction

Each of these theories seeks to explain why people don't make optimal decisions, or at least choose the option that would provide the biggest benefit. Essentially, behavioral economics describes how and why people make irrational decisions and aren't capable of behaving any other way.

What Influences Our Decisions?

In the ideal world of economists, people always make rational decisions based on perfect information. But it turns out that things other than pure information factor into our decision-making, leading to choices that don't make economic sense.

Factors that affect economic decision-making include:

- **Cognitive bias:** having feelings and reactions (that we may not be aware of) can trigger biases to things like the color of a logo or a company name
- **Herd mentality:** being influenced by what everyone else is doing, like "best seller" banners on Amazon
- **Choice architecture:** presenting information and products in specific ways can manipulate decision-making, like candy displays right next to checkout at the store

- **Bounded rationality:** making decisions based on only the information people have, even when that information is incomplete—such as when choosing stocks to invest in based on information from social media rather than researching a company and its prospects
- **Heuristics:** taking shortcuts to make decisions rather than going through a longer, more rational, and information-based process, like only buying products that are on sale
- **Sunk cost fallacy:** being reluctant to abandon something because you're already heavily invested in it with time or money, such as sticking with a hobby you don't enjoy because you've already bought supplies

Any of these, either individually or combined, can lead to choices that don't make sense from an economics perspective. Sellers that understand these factors use them to steer customers toward products and services they may not need or want but will buy based on behavioral economics.

CAPITALISM VERSUS SOCIALISM

Adam Smith and Karl Marx Duke It Out

Today, traditional economies are few and far between, command economies are waning, and pure market economies are nonexistent. What does exist is a variety of command and market systems—in effect, economic hybrids. The two most common economic hybrids are socialism and capitalism. Imagine an economic continuum with a pure command economic system on the left and a pure market system on the right. If you were to arrange modern nations along this continuum, toward the far left would be places like North Korea and Iran, in the middle would appear many western European and Latin American nations, and to the right would appear many former British colonies, such as the United States, Australia, and Hong Kong. For all practical purposes, those nations on the left were described in the discussion on command economies. However, the middle and the right of the continuum represent the dichotomy of socialism and capitalism.

Capitalism and Democracy

Do not confuse capitalism with democracy. The two do not necessarily go together. India is the world's largest democracy, but it is considered a socialist economy. Hong Kong has never really experienced democracy and yet it is the epitome of capitalism.

The difference between socialism and capitalism lies in the degree of government influence and state ownership of the factors of production. Countries that are capitalist rely on market prices for efficient product allocation, promote the private ownership of economic resources, and leave most economic decisions to individuals. They do, however, permit the government to regulate markets, preserve competition, subsidize and tax firms, enforce private contracts, and redistribute income from workers to non-workers.

For example, the US government creates rules for the labor market, breaks up monopolies, subsidizes some farmers, taxes polluters, hears cases involving breaches of contract, and collects Social Security taxes.

In socialism, the government takes a much more active role in the economy. Although individuals are allowed private property, the state may own firms in key industries and regulate even more economic decisions than in capitalism. In France, it is not uncommon for the government to take a major stake in French companies, if not outright own them. The French labor market is more heavily regulated than its American counterpart. In 2006, French students poured into the streets, protesting the fact that the government was being pressured by French firms for the right to fire employees at will during their first two years of employment. Compare this to the United States, where there is no guarantee of employment.

The Anti-Socialist Prime Minister

British Prime Minister Margaret Thatcher is credited with reversing the United Kingdom's drift toward socialism. With the end of World War II, the British had moved toward socialism with the nationalization of several key industries. While in office, Thatcher began the process of privatization, where state-owned companies were sold to private shareholders.

More often than not, socialist countries manage the prices of many goods and services. The EU monitors and regulates prices on such things as pharmaceuticals, telephone service, and food. Also, socialist countries are more active in taxing in order to redistribute income from workers to non-workers. Germany is well known for its generous cradle-to-grave social welfare system that promises care for its citizens. The German welfare state is financed by a redistributive tax system that many Americans would find intolerable. As of 2023, the highest marginal tax rate on personal income in Germany was 45% compared to the United States' rate of 37%.

ADAM SMITH, KARL MARX, AND HUMAN NATURE

According to John Maynard Keynes, "The ideas of economists and political philosophers, both when they are right and when they are wrong, are more powerful than is commonly understood. Indeed the world is ruled by little else. Practical men, who believe themselves to be quite exempt from any intellectual influences, are usually the slaves of some defunct economist." Keynes's insight into the influence of economic thought on the lives of people can be seen in the various economic systems that have developed over time. In one camp are those who would have the state as the primary caretaker of the people. In the other are those who believe that the problem of scarcity can only be addressed through individual economic freedom.

Karl Marx said, "From each according to his ability, to each according to his needs." Marx envisioned an economy where the problem of scarcity was addressed through the complete redistribution of wealth and income, from the owners of land and capital to the workers. In his utopian vision, social justice, economic equality, and relief from scarcity would be achieved when society was organized in such a way that all were equal regardless of their level of productivity.

According to Adam Smith, "It is not from the benevolence of the butcher, the brewer, or the baker, that we expect our dinner, but from their regard to their own interest. We address ourselves, not to their humanity, but to their self-love, and never talk to them of our own necessities, but of their advantages." Adam Smith had a different vision of society. In his view, productivity was the determinant of wealth, and rational self-interest was the motivating force that would provide society a means of escape from scarcity. Adam Smith believed that when society harnessed the power of self-interest, the greatest good could be accomplished.

These two men had two very different ways of addressing the fundamental problem of scarcity. Which do you think better captures human nature? If you believe that people are basically good and seek to serve one another, then the ideas of Marx ring true. However, if you believe that people are at heart selfish and pursue their own ambition, then the words of Adam Smith might appear more valid. Regardless of what you believe, both Smith and Marx have managed to influence society in ways that are still evident today.

BARTER AND THE DEVELOPMENT OF MONEY

Have You Got Change for a Cow?

Of all humankind's inventions, money stands out as one of the most widespread and useful. A day probably does not go by that you don't use it or think about it. It's hard to imagine a time when people didn't have money, and it can be scary to imagine what your life would be without it. From barter to shells to coin to paper to digital, the story of money spans much of human history.

BARTER

Before money was invented, and in times when money was either worthless or extremely scarce, barter was used as a means for people to get what they needed or wanted. Barter is simply the act of exchanging one good or service for another good or service. An example of barter is when a farmer trades a dozen chicken eggs with a baker for a fresh loaf of bread. Although barter was more common in the past, it still exists today.

Barter is not without its downsides. Obviously, trade will not occur unless both parties want what the other party has to offer. This is referred to as the double coincidence of wants. In the example of the farmer and baker, if the baker has no need or desire for eggs, then the farmer is out of luck and does not get any bread. However, if the farmer is enterprising and utilizes their network of village friends, they might discover that the baker needs some new cast iron trivets for cooling their bread, and it just so happens that the blacksmith needs a new lamb's wool sweater. Upon further investigation, the farmer discovers that the weaver has been craving an omelet for the past week. The farmer will then trade the eggs for the sweater, the sweater for the trivets, and the trivets for a fresh-baked loaf of bread. Whew! There has got to be an easier way to do things.

THE DEVELOPMENT OF MONEY

The previous example illustrates the need for a more efficient means of exchanging goods and services. As a result of the downsides to barter, cultures in different times and places eventually developed money.

Functions and Characteristics of Money

Regardless of the form it takes (gold bar, dollar bill, oyster shell), money is anything that functions as a medium of exchange, store of value, or standard of value. Money acts as a:

- Medium of exchange when it is being used for the purpose of buying and selling goods or services
- Store of value when you get it today and are still able to use it later
- Standard of value when you are using it to measure how much a good or service is worth

Money works best when it has the following characteristics: portability, durability, divisibility, stability, and acceptability.

- **Portability** refers to the ease with which money can be carried from place to place.
- **Durability** means that when you forget to remove it from your pocket before doing the laundry, you do not wind up broke.
- **Divisibility** means your money can be broken into smaller units and end up finding its way between the cushions of your couch.
- **Stability** exists when money's value does not vary too much (a dollar today buys pretty much the same amount of something as it did last week and will next week).
- **Acceptability** means people agree that the money represents what it is supposed to represent and are willing to exchange goods and services for it.

Nonportable Money

The Pacific island of Yap is known for its money, which is decidedly not portable. Large, rounded stones weighing up to hundreds of pounds are used as a medium of exchange. If you plan on visiting Yap, wait until you are there to exchange your currency because it will not fit under the seat or in the overhead compartment of an airliner. Though, nowadays, people from Yap use USD.

The Evolution of Money

Across time and cultures, many things have served as money, including salt, tobacco, shells, large stones, precious and nonprecious metals, leather, and cigarettes, to name a few. Money can be a commodity in itself, a representation of a commodity, or a completely abstract symbol of value.

Commodity Money

When relatively scarce minerals, metals, or agricultural products are used as a means of exchange, they are considered commodity money. Gold and silver struck into coins are examples of commodity money. An advantage of commodity money is that it can be used for purposes other than money. In the 1980s, many women adorned themselves in jewelry featuring gold coins, such as the Chinese Panda or the Canadian Maple Leaf. British colonists in North America not only smoked tobacco, but they also used it as money. Roman soldiers were sometimes paid in salt, then called *salarium,* which is where the word "salary" comes from. On the other hand, a commodity's usefulness also makes it disadvantageous to use it as money. If a country is dependent upon using a commodity for its money and as a resource, then money may be too precious to spend.

Representative Money

Representative money developed as an alternative to commodity money. One of the properties of gold is its high density. Transactions requiring large amounts of gold would have been unpleasant due to it being extremely heavy and difficult to transport. Goldsmiths offered a solution to this problem. They issued receipts for gold they had on deposit, which lead to the creation of representative paper money. Instead of trading the physical gold, all people had to do was trade the receipts for the gold. Whenever they wanted the actual gold, they could redeem their receipts. After years of acceptance, people became more comfortable with the idea of representative paper money and the concept stuck.

Inconvertible Fiat Money

Because people were already familiar with representative paper money, the next step in the evolution of money was not all that difficult to understand. Why bother making the paper money redeemable in anything? Several times in history, the convertibility of representative money into gold or silver had been halted because of war or other crises. In 1933, President Franklin Delano Roosevelt signed an executive order that transformed the dollar from being a form of representative money into what is called inconvertible fiat. Inconvertible fiat refers to both paper and virtual money that is intrinsically worthless and is not redeemable or backed by some real commodity. It is money because the government says so and we are willing to accept it. The US dollar, the euro, the pound, the yen, and most other world currencies meet the definition of inconvertible fiat.

The Gold Standard

Under a gold standard, money is backed by a fixed amount of gold. You could actually trade your money for gold. The gold standard allows a country to only print as much currency as there is gold to back it up, preventing overprinting and devaluation. The downside: It acts as a limit on economic growth. As an economy's productive capacity grows, so should its money supply. Because a gold standard requires that money be backed in gold, the scarcity of the metal constrains the ability of the economy to produce more capital and grow.

INCONVERTIBLE FIAT EXPLORED

Welcome to the Matrix

The inconvertible fiat standard that exists today addresses the weakness of the gold standard. The gold standard's major disadvantage is that it acts as a limit on economic growth. According to economist Adam Smith, wealth is not a function of how much gold or silver a country has, but is rather the sum of all the goods and services an economy produces. It makes sense that the amount of money an economy has should in some way reflect its capacity to produce wealth. As businesses expand, they require more money in order to purchase the tools, factories, and equipment necessary to meet both their productive needs and the demand for their goods and services. Because it is not backed by anything real or tangible, the money supply is able to grow as the economy grows.

MONEY:
EVERYONE'S IMAGINARY FRIEND

This flexibility explains why the inconvertible fiat standard persists. But remember that inconvertible fiat is only money because the government says it is and people agree. For people to agree, they must have confidence that the money won't suddenly become worthless or the government backing it won't topple tomorrow. So that people do not lose confidence in the money supply, the central bank of a country must carefully control its availability so that it does not become too plentiful or too scarce.

Promises, Promises

Money is debt. The US dollar is a promise to pay from the US Federal Reserve to the holder. You might ask, "A promise to pay what?" The answer is another dollar.

When you stop to think about it, the inconvertible fiat standard sounds like science fiction. Today's money is intrinsically worthless and is only redeemable for more of the same. The system works because the government says so and everyone collectively believes it. Money is backed by nothing more than faith. When you think about direct deposit, online bill payments, debit cards, and checks, the idea of money is weirder still. You work, pay your bills, buy your groceries, and manage to survive and even thrive in the economy, yet you can go for days or weeks without even touching, seeing, or smelling money. Money is imaginary. Ponder your bank account. There are not little stacks of dollar bills sitting in the bank vault with your name on them. Instead, checking and savings accounts are nothing more than information stored on computers.

LOSING FAITH AND COLLECTIVE DESPAIR

Because money is backed by faith, anything that erodes that faith is destructive to it. One of the biggest destroyers of money, or at least of the value that money represents, is inflation. Inflation is ultimately caused by too much money in circulation. This excess money drives up prices and makes most things more expensive. Under a gold standard, people's expectations of inflation are held in check, and that not only leads to greater price stability, but also serves to stabilize employment and the economy as a whole. With a gold standard, money has to be backed by actual gold sitting in a bank somewhere. This prevents the government from overprinting its money, greatly reducing the chance for inflation to creep into the economy, and also acts as a check against governments borrowing too heavily.

Overprinting is dangerous because it causes the money to lose value and is therefore highly inflationary. During the interwar period, the German Weimar Republic overprinted their currency, and this led to rampant inflation and financial ruin. When the money is inconvertible fiat, the checks and balances inherent in the gold standard do not exist.

Overprinting and counterfeiting pose a serious threat to any money supply. Counterfeit money, which is illegally produced currency that looks the same as actual government currency, leads to an uncontrolled increase in the money supply, threatening the overall economy and decreasing the trust in physical currency.

In response to these dangers, governments are constantly coming up with new ways to better secure their money and make it more difficult to counterfeit.

MONEY SUPPLY MEASURES: M1 AND M2

This strange stuff called money is managed and measured by the Federal Reserve (the Fed), a system of federal banks and overseeing committees in the United States. There are two primary measures that the Fed uses when describing the money supply: M1 and M2.

- The M1 measurement is composed of all of the checking account balances, cash, coins, and traveler's checks circulating in the economy.
- The M2 is composed of everything in the M1 plus all savings account balances, certificates of deposit, money market account balances, and shares in retail money market mutual funds.

The M1 is mainly used as a medium of exchange, whereas the M2 is used as a store of value. The M2 is larger and less liquid than the M1.

Noncirculating "Money"

The currency and coin inside of a bank is not counted in the M1. Why not? Because it's not money until you walk out of the bank. So technically, it is inaccurate for a bank robber to demand money while in a bank.

Changes in the M1 and M2 are monitored by the Fed and act as indicators of economic activity. Sudden changes in the ratio of M1 to M2 might indicate either imminent inflation or recession. In general, if the M1 grows faster than the combined rate of labor force and productivity growth, then inflation will result. If, however, the M2 were to suddenly grow at the expense of M1 because people are saving and not spending, then that would tend to indicate that the economy is headed toward recession.

THE TIME VALUE OF MONEY AND INTEREST RATES

Carpe Diem!

Economists observe that money's value is affected by time: a dollar today is worth more than a dollar tomorrow. This has to do with opportunity cost and inflation. If you lend your friend the money in your wallet, your opportunity cost is the sacrifice of its immediate use. When your friend eventually pays you back, the money will have lost purchasing power due to inflation. For example, the chair that cost $50 when you loaned the money might cost $55 two years later when your friend pays you back, meaning not only were you unable to buy the chair when you first needed it, but it will cost you more to buy it now. There is also the risk that your friend will move to Costa Rica and "forget" to pay you back.

As a result, when people lend money, they often ask to be rewarded with an additional payment—interest—to offset the opportunity cost and inflation. When you deposit money in your savings account, you expect to earn interest for the same reason. Otherwise you would just stuff the money under your mattress.

PRINCIPLES OF INTEREST

Interest is nothing more than a payment for using money. An interest rate is the price of using money. What determines this price? It helps to think of an interest rate as a set of blocks stacked upon each other. These blocks include cost, expected inflation rate, default risk premium, liquidity premium, and maturity risk premium. Let's look at each of these more closely.

Basic Interest Rate

The first block represents the opportunity cost of using money. Some people will readily forgo the immediate use of their funds in order to receive interest. Others might be unwilling to sacrifice the immediate use of their money. In the absence of inflation or risk, the interest rate that equates the level of saving to the level of borrowing is the basic interest rate or real interest rate.

In other words, if you're willing to forgo the opportunity to use your money for a 2% interest payment (also called a return), then that would be the basic interest rate for the money you're lending. As you can imagine, the real interest rate varies from place to place and time to time. If most people are more interested in spending their money now than in forgoing its use to earn interest, the interest rate will have to rise to make them change their thinking.

The Inflationary Past

Many older Americans can remember a time in the late 1970s and early 1980s when interest rates on loans like home mortgages were as high as 20%. Compared to today's low rates, that is quite a difference. The explanation for the difference is inflation. Interest rates include a premium for inflation. So even though your savings are earning a much lower rate today, when you adjust for inflation, the differences pretty much disappear.

Expected Inflation Rate

While the basic interest rate of 2% may repay you for your opportunity cost, it doesn't account for inflation, which will eat away at that return. So, the second block of interest represents the cost of expected inflation. Assume that inflation has been stable for years at a rate of 3% and people are pretty confident that it will remain at 3%. A lender or investor will cover the cost of expected inflation by adding 3% to the 2% real interest rate, to arrive at a nominal interest rate of 5%. The nominal interest rate is the basic rate that an investor or lender will charge for the use of money.

Default Risk Premium

If there is a chance that the loan or investment will go bad, then it makes sense to add another block to the stack. This third block is referred to as default risk premium. The bigger the risk of default or nonpayment, the bigger the block, and the bigger the total nominal interest rate. Someone with a track record of paying back loans in a timely fashion will be considered less risky to loan money to than someone who has a spotty record of paying back loans, and will thus pay a lower total interest rate.

Liquidity Premium

If there is a chance that the investment or loan will be difficult to turn around and sell to another lender or investor, like a ten-year car loan, another interest block is added. This is because there's money to be made in buying and selling loans but not so much when those loans are for non-liquid commodities. Not many people are willing to assume the risk of buying a loan that is backed by a fully depreciated asset, such as a car at the end of a ten-year loan. This fourth block is referred to as a liquidity premium. Commodities that are difficult to turn into cash demand a higher interest rate.

Maturity Risk Premium

One final block is added for maturity risk. As time passes, there is a chance that interest rates will increase. If this happens, the value of the investment decreases, because who would want an investment that earns only 2% when you can get a similar one that earns 4%?

So, here's an example of how an interest rate is calculated: The real interest rate is 2% and the inflation rate is 3%, which combine to form a 5% nominal interest rate. Assume the default risk premium is 4%, the liquidity premium is 2%, and the maturity risk premium is 1%. The total nominal interest rate would stack up to 12% (2% + 3% + 4% + 2% + 1%).

A BRIEF HISTORY OF BANKING

Est. 2000 B.C.E.

Hushed tones, cool marble counters, the smell of cash, pens chained to tables stocked with blank deposit slips, solid steel doors with impressive locks, velvet-lined cords directing customers to the appropriate teller—a bank is an important place. Banks are everywhere. In the time it takes to walk from one Starbucks to another, you'll pass at least a few banks! From small towns to large cities, the ubiquity of banks reveals their importance to the economy. Despite being maligned of late, banks are an integral part of the economy. Without them, capitalism would not function.

EARLY BANKING

The roots of banking can be traced to the earliest civilizations. The Egyptians and early societies of the Middle East developed the prototype upon which modern banking is based. Agricultural commodities were stored in granaries operated by the government, and records of deposits and withdrawals were maintained. Ancient civilizations introduced money changers, who would exchange currency from different countries so that merchants, travelers, and pilgrims could pay taxes or make religious offerings.

In the Renaissance era, Italian city-states were home to the first banks, which financed trade, the state, and the Catholic Church. In order to avoid the Church's prohibition against usury (charging interest), the bankers would lend in one currency but demand repayment in another currency using an instrument called "bill of exchange." Profit was thus earned by using different exchange rates at the time the loan was made and when it was repaid. The successes of the Italian bankers induced a spread of banking further across the continent. In England, goldsmiths were responsible not only for storing gold and issuing receipts, but also for developing what is now termed fractional reserve banking. By issuing more receipts than there was gold on deposit, the goldsmiths increased the profit potential of the banking industry.

From the time of the American Revolution to the Civil War, the United States saw an expansion of relatively unregulated banking that helped finance the growth of the young republic. Modern banking in the United States traces its origins to the National Bank Act of 1863, which gave the government a means to finance the Civil War.

THE FUNCTION OF BANKS

Banks serve a variety of functions in the economy. They act as safe places for people to store their wealth, they help to facilitate trade by providing alternative methods of payment, but most important, they bring together savers and borrowers. Each of these functions is critical to the smooth operation of the economy.

By providing their customers with check-writing privileges, debit cards, credit cards, and cashier's checks, banks help to facilitate trade. With multiple means of access to stored wealth, consumers are able to make purchases more often and in more places. This allows businesses to employ more land, labor, and capital, which in turn results in a fully employed economy.

The most important function of banks is acting as an intermediary between savers and borrowers. Banks induce people to save their money by offering to pay interest. These savings are then lent to borrowers at an interest rate higher than that paid to savers, allowing the bank to profit. The saver benefits because they earn interest on a safe, liquid financial investment. The borrower benefits by having access to a large pool of funds. This is important to the economy because borrowers can now purchase durable goods or invest in capital or housing, which creates jobs and leads to economic growth.

HOW BANKS CREATE MONEY

Contrary to popular belief, most money is not created on government printing presses. When banks accept deposits and make loans, money is created. To understand how this works, you have to know some basic accounting principles.

Balance Sheets

A balance sheet compares the assets a bank owns with the liabilities it owes. If you have never taken a course in accounting, then you might not be familiar with the following equation: Assets = Liabilities + Equity. If you haven't fallen asleep yet, please bear with me through the following explanation:

- A bank's assets include everything the bank owns: buildings, equipment, loans to customers, Treasury securities, vault cash, and reserves.
- The liabilities of a bank include everything the bank owes: customers' deposits and loans from either other banks or the Fed.
- Equity, or a bank's financial capital, is the ownership interest in the bank.

Using the equation, a bank with (for example) $1 million in assets and $500,000 in liabilities would have $500,000 in equity. Additionally, changes in a bank's liabilities can create an equal change in a bank's assets. For example, if customers deposit $100,000 in a bank (a liability), then the bank's reserves increase by $100,000 (an asset). On the other hand, if customers withdraw $25,000, then bank reserves are reduced by $25,000 as well.

Capital Requirements Defined

Banks are required by law to maintain capital requirements. Historically, this is actual cash money (capital) that a bank must keep on hand to conduct its operations, usually a ratio that is related to the riskiness of its loans. The purpose is to ensure that the bank is able to pay depositors if some of the bank's borrowers cannot repay their loans.

Bank Reserves

Bank reserves are funds that are either available for lending or held against checkable deposits. The reserves available for lending are called excess reserves and those held against checkable deposits are called required reserves. Required reserves are held either as cash in the bank's vault or are deposited in the bank's reserve account with the Fed.

In the United States, the required reserve ratio, set by the Fed, is the percentage of checkable deposits that a bank cannot lend. For large banks, the required reserve ratio was 10% for decades. Then COVID-19 hit. In March 2020, the required reserve ratio was lowered to zero, allowing banks more lending flexibility in an effort to save the economy. In theory, this means that banks don't have to keep any cash on hand, but practically speaking most keep at least some available to cover things like depositor withdrawals.

The Abracadabra Part

Money is created when the bank continues to lend its excess reserves. For example, a $100,000 checking deposit generates an increase in excess reserves of $100,000. If the bank lends the full $100,000 to a customer who in turn purchases a recreational vehicle, the seller of the vehicle might then deposit the $100,000 in the bank.

What happened to the checkable deposit balance in the bank? It grew from $100,000 to $200,000 in a short period of time. Money was created. The process does not stop with just this transaction. You can see that the bank now has $100,000 in new deposits, more money for it to lend. This process continues until all excess reserves are loaned out.

The Money Divider

Just as easily as money is created, money can also be destroyed (the horror!). Money is destroyed when customers withdraw balances and pay off loans. Consider the following example. If Maria writes a $10,000 check to pay off her car loan, checkable deposits are reduced by $10,000, and the money supply shrinks. What's good for you personally may not be so good for the economy.

BANKS AS A SYSTEM: REGULATION AND DEREGULATION

You Scratch My Back and I'll Scratch Yours

Banks work together as a system in bringing together savers and borrowers. They accomplish this by lending and borrowing directly from each other. Sometimes banks may have excess reserves, but businesses or households may not be willing to borrow. Assume that Bank East is holding excess reserves, but has no opportunities to lend in its region. Bank West has no excess reserves, but has businesses and consumers clamoring for loans. Bank West can borrow from Bank East in the fed funds market (a platform for banks to borrow money overnight from other banks that have more reserves) and provide loans for its customers. Bank East profits by earning the fed funds rate (a target interest rate set by the Federal Reserve that banks charge other banks for overnight borrowing), and Bank West profits by earning the higher interest rate it charges its customers. Everyone is happy.

HELPING A POOR BANKER OUT

If a bank is low on reserves (at times when the reserve requirement is greater than zero) and will not fulfill their daily reserve requirement, they are able to borrow from other banks overnight in the fed funds market. For example, assume that Acme Bank has a customer who withdraws her entire life savings at the end of the business day so she can run off to Cozumel with her next-door neighbor. Because banks do not hold reserves against savings deposits, this might leave Acme Bank without the required reserves it must hold against checking deposits (when that requirement is more than zero). Roadrunner Bank, however, may have excess reserves available only earning minimal interest in their reserve account with the Fed. For Roadrunner Bank, it is profitable to lend its excess reserves to Acme Bank at the higher fed funds rate.

BANK RUNS

Bank runs or bank panics have occurred multiple times throughout American history. Because banks operate with far less than 100% required reserves (typically 1%–10%), it is possible that if enough customers demand their account balances on a single day, the bank will not be able to meet the demand. This is what happened to Silicon Valley Bank (SVB) in March 2023, followed immediately by Signature Bank and then by First Republic Bank in May 2023. The banks became insolvent and the customers, unable to withdraw their funds, were temporarily broke.

SVB marked the largest US bank failure since 2008. A trifecta of events led to the infamous bank run: poor management decisions, heavy investment losses, and a social media storm. When customers couldn't access their funds, the California Department of Financial Protection and Innovation shut down the bank.

The SVB collapse infected other banks. Less than forty-eight hours later, Signature Bank customers, spooked by the fall of SVB, demanded their money, sparking another bank run. That bank was also shut down by regulators. A few weeks later, First Republic started feeling that pain. By May 1, the bank had failed: the third bank failure in 2023, and the second largest in United States history.

What causes customers to demand their account balances all at once? Fear, whether based in truth or not. Many bank panics have been caused because of rumor or speculation about a bank's financial health. If enough people believe the rumor, they will logically want to withdraw their funds and move them to another financial institution or stuff them under the mattress. Once the line starts forming at the bank's door, other customers will notice and the rumor will spread. Banks can avert a run if they are able to borrow from other banks and provide their customers' balances. However, if the speculation or rumors are pervasive, then banks may become unwilling to lend to each other. When this happens, it sparks even more speculation, and could, at least in theory, create a run on the entire financial system. Though this hasn't happened since the Great Depression, it could happen the next time major banks fail.

BANK REGULATION AND DEREGULATION

Prior to the Civil War, banks were chartered by the states and were capable of issuing their own currency. In response to the government's need for revenue to pay for the war, Congress passed the National Bank Act of 1863, which created federally chartered banks capable of issuing the new national currency and government bonds.

Money Talks

bond
A security that is a promise from a borrower to pay a lender on a specified date with interest.

To ensure liquidity in case of a crisis, larger banks accepted deposits from smaller banks that could be withdrawn in case the smaller banks experienced a bank run. The system was premised on the notion that a small bank run could be handled by tapping into a much larger bank's reserves. However, the system failed to recognize the possibility that a small bank run could create a contagion that would lead to a systemic run on the banks.

Bank Regulations Since the 1900s

A widespread bank panic in 1907 led Congress to pass the Federal Reserve Act of 1913, which created the modern Federal Reserve System, America's version of a central bank. The Fed serves as the nation's chief bank regulator. The Federal Reserve Board of Governors regulates member banks while the Federal Reserve district banks supervise and enforce the board's regulations. Unfortunately, the Fed did not respond appropriately to the run on banks that occurred during the Great Depression. Instead of providing needed liquidity, the Fed dried up credit, prolonging (at least in some economists' opinion) the Depression.

Another test of the banking system came in the 1980s with the savings and loan crisis. Aggressive lending (meaning, lending money to people who generally wouldn't qualify for those loans by the savings and loan industry) and lax underwriting (not confirming or overlooking information in loan applications) led to a series of savings and loan failures. Similar to the FDIC (Federal Deposit Insurance Corporation, which insures bank deposits of up to $250,000 per customer), the Federal Savings and Loan Insurance Corporation (FSLIC) paid depositors whose institutions had failed. The American taxpayer was ultimately the loser as billions were spent to clean up the financial mess and refund depositors.

In 2010, on the heels of the 2008 financial meltdown, President Obama signed the Dodd-Frank Act into law. That put in place stricter regulations for banks with assets of at least $50 billion. The new rules included stress tests, minimum capital levels, and liquidity plans.

Throughout the twentieth century, the American economy grew and industry began to increase in size and importance. Local and regional firms were competing against national firms. Bank regulation led a large number of small banks in the US, while other countries continued to have fewer but bigger banks. The banking sector effectively lobbied for deregulation in order to grow and compete at a national and even international level.

Bank Deregulation

The deregulation of banking that occurred in the late twentieth century allowed banks to operate nationwide and also allowed them to expand the level of services they provided. Eventually certain regulations were repealed and banks engaged in the business of speculative investment. As the walls separating traditional banks from bank-like institutions came down, the seeds for another financial crisis were sowed. And as the line between banks and other financial institutions has blurred, the task for lawmakers is to create a regulatory framework that encompasses all bank-like activities.

Not surprisingly, the banks complained about Dodd-Frank, and SVB was one of the most vocal. In 2018, President Trump rolled back those tighter regulations on "smaller" banks by increasing the asset threshold from $50 billion to $250 billion. The Congressional Budget Office warned that the new threshold made it more likely that banks with between $100 billion and $250 billion in assets would fail. That came to pass in 2023, with the failures of SVB, Signature, and First Republic.

SUPPLY AND DEMAND: MARKETS

Horse-Trading 101

You're watching the news when someone says, "Higher gas prices should lower demand." How do you evaluate a statement like that? This guy is on TV, so he must know what he's talking about, right? Don't be so sure. Many intelligent individuals throw around economic arguments using economic terminology and may even sound convincing, but there is a lot of bad economics going around! To have a good understanding of economics, you must have a grasp of supply and demand. The concepts are central to even the most complex of economic arguments, yet they are easily misunderstood.

WHAT'S A MARKET?

Markets are places that bring together buyers and sellers. However, markets do not have to be physical places. Markets exist whenever and wherever buyer and seller interact, be it a physical location, via mail, or over the Internet. Several conditions must be met in order for markets to function efficiently. Typical conditions for an efficient market include a large number of buyers and sellers acting independently according to their own self-interest, perfect information about what is being traded, and freedom of entry and exit to and from the market.

A large number of participants in the market ensures that no one buyer or seller has too much influence over the price or the amount traded. It is obvious that if there is a single seller or single buyer, they will be able to exercise considerable influence over prices. For example, Walmart has what is called monopsony power over several producers.

Because Walmart is the sole retailer for these producers, it is able use that power to influence the price it pays. In competitive markets, no one producer or consumer exercises that level of influence.

Money Talks

monopsony and *monopoly*
A monopsony is when there's basically only one buyer for a product. A monopoly is when there's basically only one seller for a product.

Perfect information implies that both buyer and seller have complete access to the costs of production and perfect knowledge of the product, and no opportunities exist for arbitrage, which is buying low in one place and selling high in another. Contrast that condition with the experience of buying a car. Chances are the seller has the bulk of information about the cost and specifications of the vehicle, whereas you deal with limited information at best in making your purchase decision.

Freedom of entry and exit into the market also increases the market's efficiency by allowing the maximum number of buyers and sellers to participate. Licensing requirements are an example of a barrier to entry. By requiring licenses to sell or produce goods and services, the government limits the potential number of sellers, resulting in less competition and higher prices.

COMPETITIVE MARKETS

A variety of factors affect supply and demand, which in turn affect price and quantity. Changes in the market for one good will create changes in the market for another good. This happens as price changes are communicated across markets. This phenomenon should be considered when policymakers attempt to influence markets, or unintended consequences can result.

How might driving an SUV contribute to starvation in Southeast Asia? Several years ago gas prices suddenly began to climb. As a result, there was considerable political pressure to alleviate the squeeze placed on the pocketbooks of many Americans. Instead of driving less or commuting, many wanted to continue their lifestyle of driving an inefficient vehicle without having to pay higher prices. According to Thomas Sowell of the Hoover Institution, politicians and many other people are fond of ignoring the aphorism "there is no such thing as a free lunch." So, here is what happened.

As gas prices increased, demand for alternative fuels increased. This increase in demand for alternative fuels was popular among corn growers who had a product called ethanol. In order to provide ethanol at a lower cost, corn growers lobbied Congress for greater subsidies. This resulted in more land being placed into corn production at the expense of other crops, namely wheat. As wheat supplies decreased and wheat prices rose, the price of the substitute crop, rice, also rose because there was now more demand for rice. Markets talk to each other. No one intended for other crop prices to be affected, but when people ignore scarcity, unintended consequences can and do occur.

Unrealistic Models Explained

Do you remember the first time you learned about atoms in science class? The teacher probably drew a sketch on the chalkboard that looked like a model of the solar system: a big nucleus in the middle orbited by a tiny electron. Later you probably learned that atoms do not actually look like the drawing on the board, but the model your teacher showed you helped you to understand atoms. In economics, when studying markets, you begin by learning something that is somewhat unrealistic, but a simple model of perfect competition will help you to understand real-world conditions.

Conditions

Certain conditions are necessary for the functioning of an efficient market: a large number of buyers and sellers each acting independently according to their own self-interest, perfect information about what is being traded, and freedom of entry and exit to and from the market. Add to this list that firms deal in identical products and that they are "price-takers" (that is, they are unable to influence price much), and you now have perfect competition.

Identical products mean that there are no real differences in the output of firms. They are all making and selling the same stuff. Think of things like wheat, corn, rice, barley, and whatever else goes into making breakfast cereal. Wheat grown by one farmer is not significantly different from wheat grown by another farmer.

Advantages of Competitive Markets

Perfectly competitive markets are what economists call allocatively efficient. Consumers get the most benefit at the lowest price without creating any loss for producers. Perfect competition is also productively efficient because, in the long run, firms produce at the lowest total cost per unit.

Economists refer to firms as "price-takers" when a firm does not set the price of its output, but instead sells its output at the market price. Remember, one outcome when markets have many different small buyers and sellers is that none are able to influence the price of the product.

SUPPLY AND DEMAND: CONSUMER BEHAVIOR

In Which Economists Define Happiness

Economists are always making assumptions about people's behavior. One assumption that seems to make sense is that people try to make themselves as happy as possible. In economics-speak, this is called utility maximization. When consumers buy goods and services, they are doing so to maximize their utility. The ability of consumers to maximize utility is constrained by the amount they have to spend; this is called a budget constraint. When it comes to consumer behavior, economists argue that consumers seek to maximize their utility subject to their budget constraint.

When studying consumer behavior, it is important to focus on marginal decisions. Suppose you are faced with a bowl of your favorite candy. Each time you benefit from consuming a piece, economists say that you are experiencing marginal utility, but you do not care what economists say because you are enjoying the candy. You might describe the feeling you are having as getting happy points. The more candy you eat, the more happy points you get. You are maximizing your utility.

If you have ever overindulged on candy, cookies, brownies, or ice cream, you know that at first the eating was enjoyable, but after a few (or a dozen), you were not quite as happy as when you started. Economists refer to this phenomenon as diminishing marginal utility. In other words, each piece of candy you eat gives you fewer happy points than the prior piece. Diminishing marginal utility is a useful concept. Throw the term around the next time you're at a dinner party and see how it goes.

Diminishing marginal utility helps to explain many of your behaviors. If one peppermint makes your breath smell fresh, then why not eat fifty? Answer: diminishing marginal utility. If exercising for one hour is good for your health, then why not exercise for twenty-four straight hours? Again, the answer is diminishing marginal utility. If a drop of perfume makes you smell nice, why not wear the whole bottle? You guessed it—diminishing marginal utility.

DEMAND

If you have ever witnessed an auction, then you might have noticed that there are many more low bids for an item than high bids. That is, people are more willing and able to pay a low price for an item than to pay a high price. This willingness and ability to buy something is referred to as demand. The fact that more people are willing to buy at lower prices than at higher prices is called the law of demand.

Three reasons explain why the law of demand exists: diminishing marginal utility, income effect, and substitution effect.

Diminishing Marginal Utility
The reason that diminishing marginal utility is an explanation of the law of demand is easy to understand. As you consume more and more of an item, each successive unit provides less utility, or happy points, than the previous unit. As a result, the only way that you will buy more of an item is if the price is lower. You consume until the marginal benefit (utility) equals the marginal cost (price). Assume that your favorite doughnut stand is offering a "buy two and get the third for half price" deal. On a normal day, you would just buy two doughnuts because a third is not worth it to you due to diminishing

marginal utility. But in the case of the deal they are offering, if they lower the price or marginal cost to the point where it is equal or less than the marginal utility or marginal benefit, it makes sense for you to purchase the third doughnut.

Money Talks

marginal utility
Marginal utility refers to the additional satisfaction consumers get when they buy one more unit of whatever they're purchasing.

Income Effect
Income effect is based on your budget constraint. As the price of a good drops, your purchasing power increases. As the price increases, your purchasing power falls. Income effect explains the logic behind discounts and sale prices. When goods go on sale at a lower price, you are able to purchase more with the same income, so that is what you do.

Substitution Effect
Substitution effect is another explanation for the law of demand. The substitution effect says that you substitute relatively less expensive items for relatively more expensive items. For example, imagine you are at the grocery store to buy food for five days' worth of meals—three chicken dinners and two dinners with beef. If the store happens to have beef on sale, you might substitute one day's chicken with beef. So what happened? The law of demand happened. Beef prices were relatively lower and you bought more beef.

Elasticity of Demand

Think about all of the things that you buy in a year. You might purchase goods and services as diverse as chewing gum, emergency room visits, and cars. Sometimes you are very sensitive to the price and at other times you are not. For example, you're more likely to shop around for a good price on a car than on an emergency room visit. Economists refer to this sensitivity to price as elasticity of demand.

- When you can delay the purchase of a good, if it has many close substitutes, or if it takes a large percentage of your income, demand is typically price sensitive or elastic.
- If, however, the purchase must be made immediately, no close substitutes exist, or the purchase does not take a significant percentage of income, demand is price insensitive or inelastic.

Compare an emergency appendectomy with a facelift. Both are surgeries, but consumer demand for these surgeries is quite different. Acute appendicitis does not wait for you to shop for the best price on surgery. Price is probably the last thing on your mind when experiencing this illness. Your demand for the surgery is inelastic. Facelifts are an entirely different matter. First, the purchase can be delayed. Next, a facelift has available substitutes, like Botox and collagen injections. Finally, because facelifts are optional and not covered by most health insurance plans, they tend to take a large percentage of a person's income. The result of this combination of factors is that, for most, facelift demand is elastic.

SUPPLY AND DEMAND: A PRICE IS BORN

Finding Common Ground for Producers and Consumers

Consumers demand, producers supply. Supply reflects producers' changing willingness and ability to make or sell at the various prices that occur in the market. If you were selling cookies or crude oil, which would entice you to produce more, a low price or a high price? If you said low price, you would quickly find yourself broke. However, if you said high price, you just might have a chance to make a profit. The law of supply states that producers are able and willing to sell more as the price increases. The reason for the law of supply is the simple fact that as production increases, so do the marginal costs. As rational, self-interested individuals, suppliers are only willing to produce if they are able to cover their cost.

ELASTICITY OF SUPPLY

Elasticity of supply is the producers' sensitivity to changes in price on the quantity they are willing to produce. The key factor in supply elasticity is the amount of time it takes to produce the good or service. If producers can respond to price changes rapidly, supply is relatively elastic. However, if producers need considerable time to respond to changes in the market price of their product, supply is relatively inelastic. Compare corn tortillas and wine. Corn tortillas are easily produced with readily available materials. If the market price of corn tortillas were to suddenly increase, producers would have little difficulty in producing more tortillas in response to the price change. Now, if the market price of Pinot Noir were to suddenly increase, winemakers would have much more difficulty responding to the price change. Vines take years to develop, grapes take time to ripen, and wine needs time to age. All of these factors give wine a relatively inelastic supply.

Money Talks

elasticity

Elasticity in economics refers to how buyers and sellers respond to changing market conditions, such as price and availability.

A PRICE IS BORN

When supply meets demand, something interesting happens. A price is born. In an efficient market, prices are a function of the supply and demand for the good or service. Instead of central planners, government officials, or oligarchs dictating artificial prices or rationing who gets what, the market relies on the impersonal forces of supply and demand to determine prices and to serve the rationing function. The pitting of consumers trying to maximize their utility against producers trying to maximize their profits is what determines the price of goods in the market and also the quantity that is bought and sold.

Supply and demand ration goods and services efficiently and fairly. Prices are efficient because they are understood by most participants in the market. If you give a child $5 and send her into a candy shop, she could figure out what she can afford without having to ask anyone for help. A price conveys much information. The price of a good communicates to consumers whether or not to purchase and to the producer whether or not to produce it. Prices are fair because they are neutral; they favor neither buyer nor seller.

FINDING EQUILIBRIUM

A market is said to be in equilibrium when at the prevailing price there is neither a surplus nor shortage of the good or service. When this condition is present, then the price is called the equilibrium or market-clearing price. Market equilibrium is the most desirable outcome because it allows for consumers to maximize utility while also allowing producers to maximize profits.

There are times when the market is not in equilibrium. Sometimes, the market price is greater than the equilibrium price.

When this happens, a surplus results. The amount producers supply is greater than the amount consumers demand. If you have ever walked past a clearance rack full of sweaters and wondered to yourself, "Who would wear that?" you are not alone. Countless others had walked past those now-surplus sweaters before they were placed on the clearance rack. They walked past because the marginal cost of the sweater to the consumer was greater than the marginal utility. The purpose of the clearance rack is to offer these sweaters at a price low enough to induce some utility-maximizing individual to purchase them.

If the market price is too low, then a shortage might result. Shortages occur when the quantity demanded is greater than the quantity supplied. When shortages occur in the market, buyers compete against each other to purchase an item and bid up the price until equilibrium is reached. Auctions take advantage of this phenomenon, and the consumer who wants the good the most gets it. How do you know he wanted it the most? He offered the most money. Prices are fair, efficient, and effective at rationing most goods and services.

CHANGES IN SUPPLY AND DEMAND

What Goes Up Must Come Down

Change in either demand or supply will cause change in both price and quantity. As price changes, producers are willing to produce more or less. Price affects the quantity producers supply, but it does not affect supply. For example, the supply of coffee is influenced by weather, land prices, other coffee producers, coffee futures, cocoa profits, and subsidies to coffee producers. The one thing that does not influence the supply of coffee is the current price of coffee. This often causes confusion, but it need not. Understand that supply refers to producers' willingness to produce various amounts at various prices, and not to some fixed quantity.

WHAT CAUSES SUPPLY TO CHANGE?

Supply is influenced by nature, the price of inputs, competition, expected prices, related profits, and government.

- Nature plays a big part in determining the supply of coffee. Rain, sunshine, temperature, and disease are obvious examples of variables in nature that will affect the coffee harvest.
- Input or resource prices have a direct influence on producers' supply decisions. Land, seed, fertilizer, pesticide, harvesting equipment, labor, and storage are just a few of the costs that coffee producers face. Supply decreases as those costs rise, making

growers less able to produce at each and every market price. Supply increases when the cost of production falls.

- The presence of more or less competition causes increases or decreases in supply. As the popularity of coffee has risen, more and more producers have entered the market. The introduction of more competition increased the quantity of coffee supplied at each market price.

- Expectations of future price increases tend to decrease supply, but expectations of future price decreases have the opposite effect. If producers expect higher prices in the future, they will be less willing to supply in the present. Coffee producers might withhold production in order to sell when prices are higher. If prices are expected to move lower in the future, producers have an incentive to sell more in the present.

- The profitability of related goods and services also affects the supply of a good like coffee. For example, coffee-growing land is also favorable for growing cocoa. If the profits are greater in the cocoa market than in the coffee market, over time more land will be pulled from coffee production and put into cocoa production.

- Government policies can also affect supply. Government can tax, subsidize, or regulate production, and this will affect supply. If Brazil wants to reduce the local production of coffee in order to restore forests, the Brazilian government can tax coffee production. This would increase the cost of production and reduce the supply. If government wants to encourage production and increase supply, it can subsidize producers—that is, pay them to produce.

- Technology and the availability of physical capital are key determinants of supply. Technological innovation has allowed producers in many different industries to increase the quantity of goods that they are willing and able to produce at each and every price.

- Increases in the amount of physical capital available relative to labor also help firms to increase output. Economists refer to this phenomenon as capital deepening. As capital deepening increases for a firm, so does supply.

Money Talks

capital

Capital in economics does not refer to money, but to all of the tools, factories, and equipment used in the production process. Capital is the product of investment.

WHAT CAUSES CHANGES IN DEMAND?

Consumer tastes for goods and services are subject to change, and when these changes happen, demand shifts. For example, in December 2023, Quaker Oats had to recall granola bars and cereals due to potential salmonella contamination. This contamination effectively reduced demand for their products. Advertising and social media can affect the taste for goods and services as well. Starbucks' Unicorn Frappuccinos is a case in point. Social media exploded with tweets, Instagram posts, and ads for the product. After seeing the beverages for the hundredth time, many people decided that they had to have one and post about it. The increase in sales was brought on by a change in consumers' tastes due to advertising and social media.

Complements and Substitutes

The price of related goods can affect the demand for a good as well. Related goods are classified as either complements or substitutes. Complements are goods used in conjunction with other goods, and substitutes are goods used in lieu of each other. Movie tickets and Junior Mints are complements. As the price of movie tickets rises, people are less willing to buy them and go to the movies. Therefore, there is less demand for Junior Mints. If ticket prices fall, the opposite occurs. Air travel and bus travel are substitutes. As the price of airline tickets falls, demand for bus tickets decreases, and as the price of airline tickets rises, demand for bus tickets increases.

Normal and Inferior Goods

Changes in consumers' incomes will lead to changes in demand. If income and demand move in the same direction, you are dealing with a normal good. If income and demand move in opposite directions, the good is considered inferior. If organic milk is a normal good and powdered milk is an inferior good, what effect will an increase in consumers' incomes have on demand for the two? Demand for organic milk increases with increased income and demand for powdered milk decreases with increased income.

Number of Buyers and Expected Prices

The number of buyers is directly related to the demand for goods and services. As the number of buyers increases, so will demand, and vice versa. You can see this with Peloton exercise equipment. During the pandemic, the customer base for home workouts skyrocketed. As people were able to resume normal activity, demand decreased.

Expected prices can have a direct influence over the demand for goods and services. If investors believe that a stock's price will increase in the future, demand for the stock increases. Likewise, if the price of a stock is expected to fall, the demand for the stock will decrease.

SUPPLY CHAIN INTERRUPTIONS
AND PANIC DEMAND

Along with lockdowns, fear, and overcrowded hospitals, COVID-19 triggered severe supply chain shortages that made it impossible for producers and consumers alike to get all the goods they needed. Those shortages were exacerbated by panic hoarding and price gouging.

Strict lockdowns in China halted production of parts and materials needed around the world, effectively causing delays everywhere along the supply chain. US manufacturers couldn't produce their products as usual, even after people returned to work.

Notable consumer shortages during the COVID-19 catastrophe included:

- Personal protective equipment (PPE)
- Hospital ventilators
- Medications (from antibiotics to acetaminophen)
- Automobile parts
- Air conditioners
- Consumer electronics (from smartphones to TVs)

Panic demand, or fear of products becoming unavailable, led to hoarding of products like hand sanitizer, toilet paper, and diapers. This created additional shortages—leading to increased demand with no supply to fill it, and higher prices on many goods.

ACCOUNTING VERSUS ECONOMICS

You Say Potato, I Say Rutabaga

An accountant asked an economist why she had chosen a career in economics over accounting. The economist replied, "I'm good with numbers, but I don't have enough personality to be an accountant." Personality differences aside, a key distinction between economics and accounting is in determining total cost and profit. To the accountant, total costs are the sum of all of the explicit fixed and variable costs of production—things like the cost of clay to make the ceramic pots you sell. Explicit costs are easily identifiable and quantifiable. The cost of overhead is a known quantity. The cost of labor can readily be calculated.

In addition, to the accountant, profits are equal to total revenue minus total cost. If your business generates $1 million in revenue (what it earns through sales) and has fixed and variable costs equal to $800,000, then your profits are equal to $200,000. Your focus will be on maximizing revenue and reducing the costs of production. This will increase your profits.

To the economist, however, total cost is equal to all of the explicit fixed and variable costs *plus* opportunity cost. Opportunity cost is an implicit cost, and it can be much harder to define and quantify than the explicit costs of production. To the economist, profits are equal to total revenue minus total cost including opportunity cost. Factoring in opportunity cost gives a clearer picture of not just whether the business is profitable but whether it is the best use of resources.

A CASE IN POINT

Imagine that you are a teacher earning $5,000 a month and decide to quit your job and start selling snow cones instead. You buy a freezer cart that you can wheel around, order all of the supplies you need, and pay the required licensing fees. Assume your total cost equals $2,000. So you get out there and start hustling snow cones, and you're actually good at it. At the end of the month, you calculate that you have earned $6,000 in total revenue.

What are your accounting profits? $6,000 in total revenue – $2,000 in total cost = $4,000 in accounting profit. What are your economic profits? $6,000 in total revenue – ($2,000 in explicit cost + $5,000 in opportunity cost) = –$1,000 economic loss. The opportunity cost is what you could have been earning as a teacher.

In this example, we knew what salary the teacher earned so we could calculate the opportunity cost more easily. But what if the situation were slightly different? Suppose the teacher was selling snow cones in the summer, not during the school year, so her teaching salary was unaffected. She might be giving up other opportunities, but perhaps it isn't clear what those opportunities would be or how much she might earn pursuing them. What's the going rate for tutoring, a common summertime pursuit for teachers? Maybe it varies from $15 an hour to $100 an hour, depending on a variety of factors. Or maybe the opportunities aren't income generating—maybe she could be lying on the beach, recuperating so she can be ready for another round of teaching in the fall.

Revenue and Profit

Many people confuse the concepts of revenue and profit. Revenue is all of the income a business earns. For a firm selling a single type of product at one price, revenue is equal to the quantity sold multiplied by the price. If you've got 100 apples that you sell for $1 each, then your total revenue, assuming you sell all the apples, is $100. Profit, on the other hand, is the income a company has left over after covering all of its costs. Revenue – Cost = Profit.

Economic profits in an industry are important because they provide firms in other industries with an incentive to employ their land, labor, capital, and entrepreneurial ability in the economically profitable industry. Economic profits draw resources to their most efficient use. In the long run, competition eliminates economic profits. Industry is most efficient when economic profits are equal to zero. At zero economic profit, there is no incentive for existing firms to leave or for new firms to enter the market. In the example just presented, the $1,000 economic loss is a signal for you to leave the snow-cone industry because your resources could be put to better use in another industry. But for the kid whose alternative is mowing lawns, making snow cones is an efficient way to use his resources as opposed to the other options available to him, so he has no incentive to leave the market.

THE PRODUCTION FUNCTION

The Only Constant Is Change

Businesses frequently have to make production decisions in response to market conditions. If the price of tea goes up, should Green Tea Inc. expect less demand for their tea bags and therefore decide not to hire a new person to fill Dwayne's spot on the line? Does a big order of tablet computers now indicate that production capacities at I Heart Electronics Inc. should be increased to deal with future big orders, or is that order just an anomaly?

Both microeconomics and macroeconomics make distinctions between production decisions in the short run and production decisions in the long run. These distinctions have very little to do with some fixed period of time, but rather are based on the ability of firms to make changes in their inputs.

THE LONG AND SHORT OF IT

The short run is defined as the period of time in which firms are able to vary *only one* of the inputs to production, usually labor. The long run is the period in which firms are able to vary all the inputs in the production process.

If you operate a restaurant, in the short run (today and next week) you can only add or subtract workers to adjust the level of production. If your place is busy, you schedule or call up more of your workers. If business is slow, you send the employees home. The long run is the period in which you are able to expand the kitchen or add new equipment. So in response to an increase in business activity, in the short run you can schedule more workers, but in the long run you can make the restaurant bigger.

A firm's short-run production decisions are based on the firm's production function. A production function shows how a firm's output changes as it makes changes to a single input, like labor.

The Stages of Production Function

The production function is divided into three distinct stages based on what is happening to the firm's output or product:

1. The first stage of a production function occurs when firms experience increasing returns. This means that as a firm adds workers, each additional worker contributes more to output than the previous worker. The additional contribution to output from each worker is referred to as marginal product. So in the stage of increasing returns, both output and marginal product are increasing. If one worker laboring alone can produce ten candles a day at the Cheerful Candle Company, but a second worker can (through the miracles of the division of labor and mass production) produce fifteen candles a day, that's an increase in output and marginal production, and an indication that the business is in the increasing returns stage.

2. The second stage of production is called diminishing returns. In this stage, as the firm increases the number of workers, output still increases, but the additional contribution of each worker decreases. By the time the Cheerful Candle Company hires its fiftieth employee, that employee may be able to produce fifteen candles a day but that level of production (while perfectly satisfactory) does not contribute more to output than the previous worker contributed. It could be by the time the Cheerful Candle

Company hires its hundredth employee, that employee could be producing less than employee number fifty but still adding to the overall bottom line (output) of the company.

3. Finally, the firm experiences the third stage of production called negative returns. In this stage, as firms add workers, both output and marginal product decrease. If you've ever worked for a large company with a lot of middle managers, you can imagine how this might happen.

CONTROLLING COSTS

Businesses strive to earn the most profits possible by trying to increase revenues and decrease costs. In a competitive environment, firms can't do much to increase revenue. If Target is selling Beautiful Brand toilet paper for $1 per four-pack, Walmart is also going to have to sell Beautiful Brand toilet paper for about $1 per four-pack. They lack pricing power. Firms do, however, have the ability to control costs, so in order to maximize their profits they try to produce at the lowest cost possible.

Money Talks

depreciation

As capital ages, its value declines because it breaks down and eventually needs replacement.

Think of it this way: If you'd like to have enough money in the bank to retire someday, you may be able to work toward getting a raise (or a better job with an increase in pay), but you may not have a lot of control over this—the company will determine how much, if any, of a raise you can get, and your ability to get a better-paying job depends on many factors. But even if you couldn't easily get an increase in salary, you probably could cut out a daily coffee and save a few bucks that way.

TYPES OF COSTS

Economists break down costs into different categories:

1. Fixed costs or overhead: Fixed costs don't change regardless of the level of production. Rent, property tax, management salaries, and depreciation are examples. Whether a factory is running at full capacity or is idle, the overhead remains the same.
2. Variable costs: Variable costs change with the level of a firm's output. Utilities, hourly wages, and per-unit taxes are representative of variable costs. As a firm's production increases, so do its variable costs.
3. Total cost: This is the sum of a firm's fixed and variable costs.
4. Profits = Revenue - Costs (Fixed and Variable).

Costs over the Long Run

In the long run, all costs are variable. Over time, firms are able to add or subtract capital, renegotiate rent, and alter management salaries. The distinction between fixed and variable costs disappears with the passage of time.

Marginal Cost of Production

The marginal cost of production is of special interest to economists. Marginal cost is the change in total cost for each unit produced, the additional cost of producing one more item. For each additional unit of output a firm produces, it incurs more variable cost and hence more total cost. This means that its marginal cost increases as well. For example, each Big Mac costs more to produce than the previous Big Mac because McDonald's had to pay for more ingredients and pay its workers more for the extra time it took to produce the additional Big Mac.

Marginal Revenue

Firms like McDonald's maximize their profits when they produce at the point where marginal cost equals marginal revenue. In other words, if a firm wants to make the largest profits it can, it will produce up to the point where the additional cost of producing one more item is the same as the additional revenue earned by producing one more item.

If the additional cost of making "one more hamburger" is $0.99 (for example) and that hamburger can be sold for $0.99, then marginal cost and marginal revenue are equal. This is the happy place economists dream of. If the additional cost of making "one more hamburger" is instead $1.29 and selling it can only generate revenue of $0.99, McDonald's will have some explaining to do to their stockholders and will probably shortly be in search of a new CEO.

PERFECT COMPETITION IN THE SHORT AND LONG RUN

Let's Pretend!

Perfect competition is the kind of hypothetical situation that economists love to talk about even though it exists in the same fairy-tale realm as unicorns and dragons. Perfect competition is the made-up idea that businesses will behave in certain ways if we stipulate that all of the businesses in a particular industry are playing on a level field. The theory of perfect competition allows economists to describe what would happen if only people would listen to them. These economics lectures usually include charts containing complicated formulas but we're omitting them here. You're welcome.

PERFECT COMPETITION IN FOUR EASY PIECES

What constitutes the aforementioned level playing field? For starters:

- Consumers and producers have perfect knowledge—they know all there is to know about the product and the market—and they make rational decisions. That means consumers are trying to maximize utility (i.e., happy points) and producers are trying to maximize profit, and both groups have all the information they need to be able to do these things.

- Businesses can enter and exit the market without barriers. Here we pretend that businesses don't have to beg venture capitalists for start-up funds or hold going-out-of-business sales.
- All producers make things ("outputs" or finished goods) that are identical and all of them have inputs (e.g., labor) that are the same. In Perfect Competition World, a pair of Keds and a pair of Dolce & Gabbana shoes are exactly equivalent and require exactly the same resources to produce.
- Lots of producers are competing in the same area, meaning that no producer (business) has pricing power—none is big enough or monopolistic enough to manage it. Everyone prices their goods in relationship to everyone else. If Blue Skies Coffee Company sells a pound of arabica coffee beans for $20, then Green Earth Coffees Inc. will have to sell their arabica coffee beans for about the same amount of money or the business won't have any buyers. Remember, in this scenario, all outputs are the same and all consumers have perfect knowledge, so they know Blue Skies coffee is just as good as Green Earth coffee.

In other words, businesses must compete against each other without any advantages (or disadvantages!). The result is that the industry sets the price rather than individual businesses, and demand is perfectly elastic. (Remember that if a good has many acceptable substitutes, the demand is price sensitive, which is another way of saying demand is elastic.)

COMPETITION AND THE SHORT RUN

For an industry, the short run is the period of time in which firms are unable to enter or exit the market because they are only able to vary their labor and not their fixed capital. That is to say, if demand plummets, a business cannot quickly reduce their fixed costs; if demand skyrockets, they cannot quickly expand to produce more. In the short run, it is possible for firms in a perfectly competitive industry to earn economic profits or even operate at a loss as supply and demand for the entire industry's output changes.

For example, assume that the glazed doughnut industry is perfectly competitive. Imagine that scientists working in New Zealand discover that glazed doughnuts, when consumed with coffee, are extremely beneficial to consumers' health. As a result of this great news, the demand for doughnuts increases. This results in a new, higher equilibrium price. Remember that the market price represents the firm's marginal revenue, so for firms in the doughnut industry, their total revenue has increased by more than their total economic cost. This means that glazed doughnut firms are earning economic profits.

Six months later, scientists in California reveal that the earlier New Zealand doughnut research was flawed, and that, in fact, consuming large amounts of glazed doughnuts with coffee might pose a risk to consumers' health. At this point, the demand for glazed doughnuts decreases below its original equilibrium. For many firms in the doughnut industry, this decrease in the market price means that they are now producing at a short-run loss, because their total revenue is less than their total cost of production.

PERFECT COMPETITION
IN THE LONG RUN

Unlike the short run, in the long run, firms are able to enter and exit the market. New firms enter the market in response to the presence of economic profits, and old firms exit the market in response to losses. To continue the doughnut example, consider how, in light of the New Zealand research, economic profits in the glazed doughnut industry would attract new firms to the industry. As new firms enter, competition increases, which means that the industry supply of glazed doughnuts increases. The increased supply reduces the equilibrium price of doughnuts and economic profits disappear.

Considering the California research, in the face of economic losses, some firms will reach the shutdown point and withdraw from the industry. This reduces competition and decreases the industry supply of glazed doughnuts. Decreased supply increases the equilibrium price in the market. In the end, fewer firms remain as the industry returns to its long-run equilibrium with zero economic profits.

FROM COMPETITION TO IMPERFECT
COMPETITION: A CONTINUUM

Perfect competition does not really exist. It is unlikely that you will find an industry in which all of the conditions for perfect competition are met. However, perfect competition provides an example with which to compare the market structures that do exist, providing a nice frame of reference.

The Evolution of Markets

The continuum of market structures can be seen as an evolution of markets. Firms may begin in a very competitive market and over time become monopolists. The late nineteenth and early twentieth centuries witnessed the rise of major trusts from once-competitive industries. Some even called for an end to "ruinous competition."

Most firms face barriers to entry, either in terms of cost or government requirements. Firms rarely deal in identical products, as they invest heavily in differentiating themselves from the competition. This ability to differentiate gives firms some ability to affect prices. In mature markets like the United States, firms tend to be large and not necessarily independent. Finally, access to information is not equally shared, so the condition of perfect information does not exist either. What you are left with is imperfect competition.

Economists classify markets according to their level of competition. On one end of the spectrum lies perfectly competitive, albeit fictional, markets. On the other end of the spectrum lies monopoly. In between you will find the market structures that are most familiar: monopolistic competition and oligopoly.

Monopolistic Competition

Monopolistic competition is a market structure very similar to perfect competition. There are many buyers and sellers, barriers to entry are minimal or at least equal for all firms, and information is readily available. However, in monopolistic competition, firms do not offer identical products, but differentiate their products from those of their competition. Product differentiation is the process by which producers are able to convince consumers that their particular product is different from other producers' products.

The industry that may come to mind when you think of monopolistic competition is fast food. The fast-food industry has many different producers competing for the dollars of many different consumers. All are welcome to start a fast-food restaurant as long as they pay the required licenses. Most producers have a good idea of what they are getting into and customers tend to understand the products quite well. Why is fast food monopolistically competitive? Product differentiation. Each firm offers a different menu. Taco Bell, Popeyes, McDonald's, and Subway all compete against each other in the fast-food market while providing customers with a variety of choices. Product differentiation is one of the reasons that new entrants are able to survive in this cutthroat industry. If you are different enough, then you might have a chance.

Monopolist Competition and Profit

Can monopolistically competitive firms maintain economic profits in the long run? No. Over time, the presence of competition will eventually erode the monopolistically competitive firm's profits. The end result is an industry with excess capacity, high cost, and no economic profits.

The problem with product differentiation is that firms must continually find ways to differentiate. This explains why firms will spend large sums of money on advertising in an effort to build brand loyalty. However, firms have limited resources, so engaging in product differentiation through advertising means that resources used in advertising are no longer available for production. As a result, industries that are monopolistically competitive do not produce as much output as they could if they were perfectly competitive.

OLIGOPOLIES AND IMPERFECTLY COMPETITIVE MARKETS

World Domination or Die!

Many of the companies with which you are most familiar do not exist in perfectly competitive markets or even in highly competitive markets. The major automobile manufacturers, airlines, telecommunications companies, food producers, and discount retailers compete in an oligopolistic market structure—that is, a market with few producers.

At a local level, many of the utilities you use are monopolies. Oligopoly and monopoly are common market structures in the United States. In the previous section, we briefly described monopolistically competitive firms. Now, let's look at oligopolies. To know how the American economy works, you need a good understanding of these imperfectly competitive market structures.

OLIGOPOLY

Oligopoly describes a market where a few large producers dominate. Unlike competitive and monopolistically competitive markets, oligopolistic firms have more pricing power. In addition, oligopoly is characterized by considerable barriers to entry because of the sheer scale of the firms. Oligopoly is often the result of once-competitive markets maturing. As monopolistically competitive firms grow and merge with other firms, fewer firms result. Oligopolies are of concern to government regulators attempting to preserve and enforce competition in industries.

Loss of Competition

Why does it matter if firms consolidate, industries mature, and markets become oligopolistic? As competition decreases, a number of negative effects occur. Prices become higher, and productive and allocative efficiency, which benefit society, are lost. Notice how these are industries where consumers tend to dislike the producers. (Has anyone ever actually loved an airline the way they love a chocolate chip cookie?) An interesting coincidence, wouldn't you say?

To determine whether a market meets the condition of oligopoly, economists calculate the Herfindahl-Hirschman Index (HHI) for the market. A relatively low index number identifies a market as competitive, and a relatively high index number indicates oligopoly. The Federal Trade Commission (FTC) and the Justice Department can use the index numbers as a way to determine whether or not to approve mergers between companies in an industry. If the merger would significantly increase the HHI, then the merger would most likely be blocked because it would reduce competition.

Regulators and economists also use concentration ratios to determine if a market is oligopolistic. The more market share is dominated by a few firms, the higher the concentration ratio. For example, if the four-firm concentration ratio is 80%, then the four largest firms have 80% of the market share. In 2022, the four-firm concentration ratio for stream services was 72.8%. It is safe to say that the streaming services industry is an example of oligopoly. By way of comparison, a perfectly competitive industry would have a four-firm concentration ratio of about 0%, and an industry dominated by a monopoly would have a one-firm concentration ratio of 100%.

What Defines an Industry?

What defines an industry for the purpose of determining concentration ratios? It depends. Today the definition of industry is becoming blurred. In the past, the newspaper industry was an industry. Today it is part of a larger industry known as the media. Even though the local paper may have 100% of the local newspaper market share, other forms of media reduce its effective share in the overall industry.

The large market share that oligopolists enjoy shapes the way they view the market. Unlike firms in more competitive market structures that behave independently of each other, the oligopolists have an interdependent relationship with each other. Because the oligopolists control so much market share, their individual decisions have considerable impacts on market prices. Knowing this to be the case, the oligopolist tends to be more aware of the competition and takes this into account when making production and pricing decisions.

COLLUSION AND CARTELS

World Domination or Die! Revisited

One of the blessings of competition is that it leads to lower prices for consumers. For the producer, however, this blessing is a curse. Low prices often mean low profits. Given a choice between competition and cooperation, profit-maximizing firms would often prefer cooperation. Regardless of what you learned in kindergarten, you do not want the businesses you buy from to cooperate because they might all decide that chocolate should cost $100 a pound or they might all agree to throttle back production to create an artificial scarcity. It's in your best interest for businesses to compete against each other to produce those low, low prices consumers like so well. Adam Smith, the father of modern capitalism, warned that nothing beneficial comes from the heads of businesses getting together, and history has proven him right.

Money Talks

cartel

A group of producers that agree to cooperate instead of competing with each other. Cartels seek higher profits for their members by collectively reducing production in order to increase prices.

COLLUSION

In the United States, firms are forbidden from cooperating to set prices or production. The abuses of the late nineteenth- and early twentieth-century trusts were the impetus for the "trust-busting" of President Theodore Roosevelt. With the Sherman Antitrust Act and later the Clayton Antitrust Act, the government prohibited outright collusion and other business practices that reduced competition. In economics, collusion means an intent to illegally conspire to cheat or defraud consumers (and others) by artificially reducing competition.

Even though it violates the law, businesses from time to time will collude in order to set prices. Colluding firms can divide up the market in a way that is beneficial for them. The firms avoid competition, set higher prices, and reduce their operating costs. Because collusion is illegal and punishable by fine and prison, executives at firms are reluctant to engage in the practice. The meetings of business leaders are almost always in the presence of attorneys in order to avoid the accusation of collusion.

FORMING CARTELS

Businesses that collude may form cartels. A cartel is a group of businesses that effectively function as a single producer or monopoly able to charge whatever price the market will bear. Probably the best-known modern cartel is the Organization of the Petroleum Exporting Countries, or OPEC. OPEC is made up of thirteen oil-exporting countries and is thus not subject to the antitrust laws of the United States. OPEC seeks to maintain high oil prices and profits for their members by restricting output. Each member of the cartel agrees to a production quota that will eventually reduce overall output and increase prices. OPEC is bad news for anyone who enjoys cheap gasoline.

Fortunately for consumers, cartels have an Achilles' heel. The individual members of a cartel have an incentive to cheat on their agreement. Cartels go through periods of cooperation and competition. When prices and profits are low, the members of the cartel have an incentive to cooperate and limit production. It is the cartel's success that brings the incentive to cheat. If the cartel is successful, the market price of the commodity will rise. Individual members driven by their own self-interest will have an incentive, the law of supply, to ever so slightly exceed their production quota and sell the excess at the now higher price. The problem is that all members have this incentive and the result is that eventually prices will fall as they collectively cheat on the production quota. Cartels must find ways to discourage cheating. Drug cartels use assassination and kidnapping, but OPEC uses something a little more civilized. The single largest producer in the cartel is Saudi Arabia. Saudi Arabia also has the lowest cost of production. If a member or members cheat on the cartel, then Saudi Arabia can discipline the group by unleashing its vast oil reserves, undercutting other countries' prices, and still remain profitable. After a few months or even years of losses, the other countries would then have an incentive to cooperate and limit production once again.

GAME THEORY

I'd Like to Buy a Vowel, Please

Economists have discovered that game theory is useful for understanding the behavior of oligopolists. Game theory looks at the outcomes of decisions made when those decisions depend upon the choices of others. Game theory is a study of interdependent decision-making.

THE PRISONER'S DILEMMA

One game that is particularly applicable to the study of oligopoly is the prisoner's dilemma. In one example of this dilemma, two men, Adam and Karl, are picked up by the police on suspicion of burglary. The chief investigator knows that she has little evidence against the men and is counting on a confession from either one or both in order to prosecute them for burglary. Otherwise, she can only prosecute them for unlawful trespass.

Upon entering police headquarters, the men are immediately separated and taken to different rooms for interrogation. The interrogator individually informs Adam and Karl that if one confesses to the crime and implicates his partner while the other remains silent, then the one who confesses will receive a two-year jail sentence while the silent partner will likely serve a ten-year sentence in a notorious prison. If both confess then they will likely each serve a three-year prison sentence.

What is the best strategy for Adam and Karl? If they could get together and collude, both would probably decide that it would be wise to remain silent and serve a one-year jail term for unlawful trespass. However, they are unable to collude, so they each must consider their options. Adam thinks to himself, "If I confess, then I'll either go to jail for two years or three years. If I'm silent, then I'll either spend a year in jail or go to prison for ten years." Karl thinks exactly the same thing. Because they are separated and have no idea what the other is doing, they both confess in order to avoid a possible ten-year prison sentence. They both end up doing three years in jail. This logical conclusion is referred to as a dominant strategy.

GAME THEORY IN BUSINESS

Some business decisions follow the same logic. Assume in an isolated small town there are only two gas stations and they are out of direct sight from each other. By law they are only allowed to change their price once a day. Each firm has two pricing options available to them. They can charge a high price or a low price. From past experience they know that when they both charge a high price, they both profit by $1,000. When one charges a high price and the other a low price, then the high-priced station earns $300 in profits while the low-priced station earns $1,200. When they both charge a low price, then profits are $750 for each.

If given the chance to collude, which strategy would they both take? Given collusion, both would agree to set a high price for gas and each would earn daily profits of $1,000. What should the gas stations do if they are unable to collude? The thinking goes like this: "If I charge a high price, I'll either earn $1,000 or $300. If I charge a low price, I'll either earn $1,200 or $750." Because the firms are out of sight from each other and have no legal way to know the other's pricing strategy, then their best course of action or dominant strategy is to set a low price, which guarantees at least $750 in profits and as much as $1,200. Just like in the prisoner's dilemma, when the players do not have the ability to collude, they select a strategy that results in an outcome that is not necessarily the one that maximizes profits.

Unlike the prisoner's dilemma, which is a one-time game, firms compete against each other day after day. Given the chance to play the "game" over and over results in something called tacit collusion. By playing a game of tit for tat, the firms can eventually reach a point where they both charge a high price and maximize their profits. How does it work?

1. Assume that on the first day, both gas stations charge a high price. Both earn profits of $1,000.
2. On the second day, one of the stations charges a high price, but the other cheats and charges a low price to earn profits of $1,200.
3. Predictably, the next day the other station retaliates and lowers its price, resulting in profits of $750 for each.
4. Eventually both gas stations come to the realization that if they both set a high price and do not cheat, they both will earn higher profits in the long run. They learn that if they cheat, their additional profit for the next day will not offset the lower profits that will ensue.

Money Talks

collusion

A secret agreement between would-be competitors to work together to gain unfair market advantages, often by fixing prices.

PRICING BEHAVIORS

Money, Money, Money

Businesses engage in many pricing (and non-price-related) competitions in order to increase their profits. The pricing behaviors they choose are related to the type of market they're in, whether an oligopoly or a monopoly.

PRICING AND OLIGOPOLIES

Interdependence leads oligopolists to behave strategically. The strategic pricing behaviors that occur in oligopoly include price leadership and price wars. In addition to these pricing behaviors, oligopolies also engage in nonprice competition. The purpose of these price and nonprice behaviors is the same, however, and that is to maximize oligopolistic firms' profits.

Price Leadership

Price leadership takes place when a dominant firm makes the pricing decision for the rest of the market. These decisions are often made public long before the new price goes into effect, and represent a form of tacit collusion. Smaller firms in the industry will usually follow suit and match the price leader's price. Price leadership offers firms an opportunity to capture a price that is higher than would occur if the firms directly competed on price. Consumers usually fare better under price leadership than they would if the firms formed a cartel, but would fare worse if the firms were highly competitive.

Price Wars

Price wars occur when firms break out of the price leadership model and begin undercutting one another's prices. Although it sounds bad, price wars are often advantageous to consumers because of the competitive prices created in the process. Some firms have been accused of financing price wars by raising prices in one part of their market in order to cut their price in another part of their market. A price war continues until the firms once again reach tacit collusion and return to the price leadership model.

Product Differentiation

While in the price leadership operating mode, firms compete on the basis of product differentiation as opposed to price. By emphasizing their product's differences and uniqueness, firms attempt to wrest market share from one another. As in the monopolistically competitive market, oligopolists engaging in nonprice competition will spend large sums on advertising. For example, the major American beer brands do not compete on price, but instead rely on nonprice competition in the form of advertising in order to gain market share from one another.

PRICING AND MONOPOLIES

On the opposite end of the spectrum from perfect competition lies monopoly. As the name suggests, monopoly is a market dominated by a single seller. In the United States, monopolies are generally not allowed to exist, and every effort is made by government regulators at the FTC to prevent their creation. The reason for this prohibition is that monopolies create a serious problem for both consumers and likely competitors in the marketplace. Despite the fact that most monopolies are undesirable, there are several good reasons for some to exist. The primary reasons for the existence of most monopolies in the United States are economies of scale, geography, government protection, and government mandate.

Money Talks

Federal Trade Commission (FTC)
An agency that enforces consumer protections, including anti-monopoly regulations, and fights anti-competitive business practices.

Price Increases

Monopoly occurs when a competitive firm eliminates all competition. Through control of key resources, mergers, and even a little help from government, once-competitive firms may find themselves in the enviable position of being a monopolist. A typical pricing behavior for a monopoly is to increase prices as much as possible.

John D. Rockefeller's Standard Oil Trust is probably the most notable American monopoly. By controlling the resource, purchasing the competition, and having political influence, Standard Oil at its height of power virtually controlled all oil production in the United States. Consumers and competitors of Standard Oil faced high prices, inefficient production, and significant barriers to entry. Eventually, the Sherman Antitrust Act was used to break up Standard Oil, and ever since, the government actively prevents further monopolies.

Now, there's a lot of talk among regulators about Meta (formerly Facebook) and its monopolistic tendencies. The FTC brought suit against the social media mega-giant in December 2020, but the case was dismissed. With WhatsApp, Instagram, and Threads under the Meta family umbrella, regulators and consumers are wary of the company's control of personal data and its lack of competition.

Price Discrimination

Because they lack competition, monopolies can engage in price discrimination to make it difficult for other firms to do business. Price discrimination is the ability to charge different customers different prices for the same good or service. For example, a railroad monopolist could charge different rates to different customers for carrying the same amount of freight. Today, thanks to the Clayton Antitrust Act, price discrimination for the most part is illegal.

Some forms of price discrimination still exist because they are seen as acceptable. You might have benefited from price discrimination the last time you went to a movie theater or flew on an airplane. Senior citizen, student, and military discounts are usually offered at theaters. Business travelers and vacationers often pay very different prices for tickets on the same flight even though they might both fly coach.

There are three main types of price discrimination. The first is first-degree, or maximum price, and it happens when companies charge the maximum price for every unit sold, though prices vary among units. This is most commonly used in service industries. The second is second-degree, or quantity-based, and it happens when businesses charge different prices for the same units based on how many a customer purchases. This includes things like bulk purchases, BOGO (buy one, get one) deals, and loyalty points. The third is third-degree, or group-based, and it happens when companies give discounts to specific groups of people. These can be age-based (like senior discounts), occupation-based (like discounts for first responders and teachers), or using other criteria (like student discounts).

MONOPOLY: THE GOOD, THE BAD, AND THE UGLY

Not Just a Board Game

Monopoly isn't always a bad thing. Then again, it isn't always a good thing. Sometimes monopoly is downright ugly, unless of course, you are the proud parent of a monopoly. When monopoly is allowed to exist, it is for a good reason. Yet, even though the reason is good, monopolies can have some negative effects. History has shown that, if left unchecked, monopolies can harm an economy.

THE GOOD

Good monopolies come in several forms depending on the type of output (good/item/service) being produced.

Natural Monopoly

The first is natural monopoly. When the average cost of production falls as a factory grows larger, then economies of scale are present. Natural monopoly exists when economies of scale encourage production by a single producer. A commonly cited example of natural monopoly is your local electrical utility. A feature of power plants that encourages natural monopoly is that as the size of a power plant increases, the cost per kilowatt hour of electricity falls. You might own a small electrical generator. Imagine the cost of operating the generator or multiple small generators just to meet your home's electrical needs. Now imagine the cost of every household in a city running on multiple portable generators. The total fixed cost of generators for the community would be quite high, and the variable cost of running gas or diesel generators would be astronomical.

Compare that situation with the one that most likely exists in your city. Instead of a multitude of portable generators, a few large nuclear power plants are able to generate electricity for the entire city at a much lower total cost. Remember that utilities are monopolies. What keeps the utility from charging a monopoly price for electricity? Government regulates the prices that utilities are able to charge their customers for electricity. By controlling prices, government encourages low-cost production while allowing the utility to experience an accounting profit on production.

Technological Monopoly

The technological monopoly is another form of monopoly that is encouraged. When a firm invents a new product or process and receives patent protection, the firm becomes a technological monopolist for that particular product. According to the US Patent and Trademark Office, patent protection lasts for twenty years from the date on which it was originally applied.

During that period of time, no other firm may develop or import the technology. The patent holder may develop or sell the rights to develop the technology to a firm that can legally operate as a monopolist. During the period of patent protection, the patent holder as a monopolist can charge a monopoly price and earn economic profits. If monopoly prices are higher than competitive prices, why is this encouraged? Patent protection encourages innovation, invention, and research and development. Without the protection, firms would have little incentive to invest billions of dollars in research knowing the firm next door could just copy the product without having made the investment, and profit nonetheless. It is in large part because of patent protection and the ability to earn monopoly profits that American and European pharmaceutical companies develop so many life-saving medications. Without patent protection, there would be little incentive for the pharmaceutical industry to pursue its research.

THE BAD?

At times the government may decide to step into the marketplace to provide a good or service. An example of government monopoly is the US Postal Service. Though it's not the only delivery company, only the US Postal Service is allowed to deliver a "letter" written on paper and delivered in a paper envelope. UPS and FedEx are in the package delivery business, even if that package is a letter written on paper and delivered in a flat paper-cardboard envelope.

Other examples of government monopoly include the various departments and agencies of the executive branch. Much of what they do and provide could be done by the private sector of the economy, but for many reasons the government has deemed them to be government functions.

Government Functions and the Private Sector

Executive branch departments and agencies carry out government functions, but that doesn't mean they can't subcontract out to private companies. In fact, there are more than ten million such contracts created every year. Examples include some student loan servicers, military contractors, and construction projects.

The arguments for and against government monopolies fall mainly on philosophical grounds. Many conservatives and libertarians are opposed to government performing the functions of private enterprise on the grounds that government is wasteful and inefficient. Those with more populist viewpoints tend to see a need for government performing some of the functions of private enterprise on the grounds that government is less wasteful and more efficient. You decide.

The Ugly

Pure, unregulated monopoly is ugly. A firm that is the sole provider of a good or service is able to prevent competition. It can charge whatever price the consumer will pay. This is the monopoly that is most harmful to society. Although one may say "to the victor go the spoils," once-competitive firms that become monopolists need to be checked by regulation or broken up into competing firms. Competition benefits society by providing a variety of goods and services at competitive prices that accurately reflect the costs of production. Pure monopoly is the opposite of this condition. Pure monopoly is one good at a price that in no way reflects the true cost of production.

The diamond monopoly of De Beers is the classic example of monopoly gone bad. De Beers at the height of its power dictated the diamond industry. By controlling the resource and coercing the wholesalers and cutters to abide by its demands, De Beers created an illusion of scarcity and value in the diamond market that allowed it to earn economic profits for over a hundred years. Now, before you sell your diamonds in disgust, you should remember that you were not coerced to buy the diamond. You bought the diamond because the benefit outweighed the cost. The problem for the buyer is that you never realized how much of the cost was De Beers's profit.

GOVERNMENT IN THE MARKETPLACE: PRICE CEILINGS AND PRICE FLOORS

But They Meant Well

From time to time, people will petition government to step in and correct perceived wrongs in the market. Often this leads to unexpected results. Without considering how people might respond to incentives, well-intentioned policies can go astray. Likewise, there are times when the market fails to provide goods or properly assign costs. This calls for government intervention to either provide or redirect incentives in such a way that the market functions better. Two approaches governments use are price ceilings and price floors.

PRICE CEILINGS

In the early 1970s, America was faced with ever-increasing food prices. As a result, people clamored for the government to step in and halt the increases. Instead of doing something about the source of the issue, the government treated the symptoms. To help households, the Nixon administration enacted price controls, such as a price ceiling on food. Retailers could not charge a price higher than the government-mandated ceiling.

A price ceiling is a legal maximum price for a good, service, or resource. At the time, the theory was that if the government imposed a price ceiling on food, prices would stop going up and everyone would have food at the price they wanted. Of course, this assumes that people do not behave like people. Remember: Prices are the result of the equilibrium of supply and demand. Also remember that these two forces are shaped by human nature.

The law of demand, which governs consumer behavior, says that as prices fall, consumers have an incentive to buy more, and as prices rise, consumers have an incentive to buy less. The law of supply, which governs producer behavior, says that as prices rise, producers have an incentive to produce more, and as prices fall, producers have an incentive to produce less.

A price ceiling encourages consumers to purchase, but discourages producers from producing. Assume that meat is currently selling for $5 per pound. Consumers feel that the price is too high, so they petition government for a price ceiling of $3 per pound. Representatives, senators, and presidents all like to get re-elected, so they cater to consumers and enact the price ceiling. The $3 price signals to consumers to purchase more, but signals to producers to produce less. The result of the price ceiling is a shortage of meat at the price of $3 per pound. At that price, more meat is demanded than supplied. Consumers got a price ceiling of $3, but many consumers did not get any meat at all.

Why Price Controls Are Inefficient

Price controls are inefficient for many reasons. One reason worth considering is that they increase the need for monitoring and enforcement. That means increased government bureaucracy, which does not come cheap. Increased government spending equals more taxes or more borrowing.

Eventually, America abandoned price controls, but it took a decade to get the underlying inflation under control. Even today you still hear of people demanding that government cap prices of various commodities. Government and consumers would be wise to learn from past mistakes and realize that attempts to control the market result in unintended consequences.

Capping Prescription Drug Prices

The Inflation Reduction Act of 2022 granted Medicare the power to negotiate and reduce prices on specific common prescription drugs. The agency will start with a roster of ten high-cost drugs in 2026 and increase to twenty drugs by 2029. Companies that refuse to cooperate will have their drugs hit with a 95% sales tax. The law also caps out-of-pocket drug costs for Medicare participants to $2,000 per year. Another key provision: The price of insulin will be capped at $35 per month for people on Medicare. The Act will reclaim $288 billion through prescription drug reforms, reducing the federal deficit. Medicare currently shells out more than $216 billion annually for prescription drugs, with just ten medications accounting for 22% of the total costs. The Inflation Reduction Act aims to get these costs under tighter control, but its full effects may not be seen for years.

PRICE FLOORS

Producers have at times called for price floors. A price floor is a legal minimum price for a good, service, or resource. Probably the best-known price floor is minimum wage. In the market for resources like labor, households supply and businesses demand. Politicians are often pressured by voters to increase minimum wage. It's believed that an increase in the minimum wage is justified because employers will pay the higher wage and maintain the same number of workers. That doesn't always happen, and research shows that other unintended consequences may occur.

While some studies suggest that increasing minimum wage effectively increases unemployment, others show no such effect. However, this policy change can negatively affect workers in other ways. One common area is worker schedules. While a company may use the same total number of labor hours, it allocates those hours differently. For example, instead of having five people work forty hours (for a total of two hundred labor hours), a company might have eight people work twenty-five hours each instead. This doesn't affect unemployment statistics, but it does negatively impact the workers with reduced hours and overall reduced pay, despite the wage increase. Reduced hours can also affect eligibility for employee benefits such as health insurance, further harming the workers.

Interestingly enough, those most in favor of increasing the minimum wage are often the same people who would be most harmed by the increase. Politicians know this now and will often pass increases in the minimum wage that keep it less than the average equilibrium wage, which is the wage point where the labor supply exactly equals demand for unskilled labor. For example, if the average market equilibrium unskilled labor wage is $14 an hour, then politicians will gladly increase minimum wage from $7.25 to $9, knowing that it will have little economic effect. Yet, they can still put a feather in their cap for "raising" the minimum wage.

GOVERNMENT IN THE MARKETPLACE: TAXES AND SUBSIDIES

The Only Certainties in Life

Government has a power that businesses envy. It is the power to coerce payment, better known as taxation. The opposite of a tax is a subsidy. A subsidy is a sum of money given by the government to an industry or business in order to help support it. Government uses taxes and subsidies not only to raise revenue or redistribute income but also to shape people's incentives and to change the marketplace.

HOW TAXATION SHAPES MARKETS

All effective governments have the power to tax. Taxes can be used as a tool of microeconomic policy. For example, if government wants to reduce the production of a certain good, they can tax the producer. This raises the cost of production for the producer and reduces the supply in the market. Reducing business taxes can also be used as a tool to encourage investment in human and physical resources. The Tax Cuts and Jobs Act of 2017 slashed the top corporate income tax rate from 35% to 21% along with delivering other business tax benefits, with politicians hoping that would spark hiring and wage increases, a nod to supply-side economic theory. While corporate investment did increase, the Act had minimal (if any) effect on boosting employment and wage growth. At the same time, the massive corporate and individual tax cuts increased the national deficit by over a trillion dollars.

The government can use taxation to raise revenue without the intention of reducing production. For example, luxury taxes on expensive goods and services raise revenue without necessarily affecting the market. If you're going to buy an expensive automobile, whether you spend $500,000 or $501,000 doesn't make a great deal of difference in your purchasing decision.

So-called "sin" taxes (taxes on nonessential but popular products like alcohol and cigarettes) are intended to generate revenue but they are also intended to reduce consumption of products considered undesirable (although not illegal) by the government. High taxes on such goods can lead to black markets in them.

HOW SUBSIDIES SHAPE MARKETS

Subsidies are used by government to encourage rather than discourage the production of certain goods and services. Subsidies have the effect of increasing the supply of the good or service and reducing its price. For example, subsidizing farm goods ensures that there is enough food and gives American farm exports a price advantage. Sometimes subsidies are given to owners of farmland to encourage them not to produce, artificially lowering production of agricultural goods to keep prices artificially high (good for farmers, not so good for consumers). Critics of farm subsidies argue that it creates inefficiency and misallocates scarce resources.

Subsidies Impede Competition

Many poor countries depend on agriculture as their chief export. A sticking point in WTO negotiations is that industrialized nations want poor nations to open up to free trade, yet industrialized nations are reluctant to end farm subsidies that make it difficult for the poor nations to compete.

Although a large number of government subsidies are agriculture related, not all of them are. Some government subsidies are indirect, such as a tax break or low-interest loan guarantee, but are still used to implement economic policies and to affect the market. Others come in the form of direct payments. Either way, they provide economic support to affect economic change. Examples include several subsidy measures implemented during the COVID-19 pandemic such as:

- Forgivable PPP (Paycheck Protection Program) loans
- Expanded EIDL (Economic Injury Disaster Loan) lending
- Economic impact payments (also called stimulus payments)
- Increased and extended unemployment payments
- Expanded child tax credit

These subsidies supported both individuals and small businesses during the pandemic in an effort to keep the American economy afloat.

CONSUMER SUBSIDIES AND THE BLACK MARKET

Black markets allow illegal trade to occur. Even food subsidies for needy families are subject to black market activity. Some receiving food assistance will willingly trade $2 in food assistance for $1 cash. They benefit because they now have the freedom to purchase whatever they want. The buyer benefits by purchasing groceries at half price. The problem with the system is that it is inefficient and creates disutility for the recipients. In a cash payment system, the recipient would benefit because he is able to buy items, like soap and toilet paper, not covered by food assistance.

The prevailing argument against a system like this is that some might not buy food with the food assistance, but instead purchase alcohol, cigarettes, or even illegal drugs. That's not what's actually happening in the vast majority of cases, but the system still has significant flaws. Consider this example: Assume that a person receiving food assistance needs toilet paper, feminine hygiene products, or diapers. She receives $100 in food stamps and immediately sells them on the black market so that she can spend $50 on other desperately needed supplies. In the end, she has $50 worth of necessities and no food. Now assume that a person receiving food assistance receives $100 cash. They purchase $50 in non-food necessities, but now have $50 left for food. They're better off and the taxpayer is better off. In addition, the cash payment system removes the black market and is much less expensive to administer.

MARKET FAILURES

Come On and Take a Free Ride

Sometimes the market fails to provide a necessary good or service or fails to properly assign costs. Economists refer to this as a market failure. Government has the capacity to step in and deal with such market failures in a variety of ways.

PUBLIC GOODS

Sometimes the market does not provide a good or service that people want. If a good is non-rival and non-excludable, the free market will probably not provide it.

- A good or service is non-rival when one person's consumption of the good or service does not diminish another's consumption of the good or service. For example, when you go to the movie theater, the presence of another person does not diminish your ability to consume the service, unless of course he has a screaming infant on his lap. A candy bar is an example of a rival good. If you eat the candy bar, then another consumer cannot.

- A good is non-excludable if the producer can't withhold it from those unwilling to pay for it. Public highways are an example of a non-rival, non-excludable good. (The movie theater is a good example of a non-rival but excludable good.) A private firm has little incentive to produce a public highway at its own cost. Therefore, it is up to government to provide these types of goods.

POSITIVE EXTERNALITY

Sometimes the production of a good or service creates a spillover or unintended benefit for someone who is neither the producer nor the consumer. Such a spillover benefit is called a positive externality. Assume you live in a typical American neighborhood. If your neighbors were to landscape and remodel their home in such a way that significantly increased its value, you also would benefit. Your home would also appreciate in value, but you paid nothing for the increase. Flu vaccines create a positive externality as well. If you're concerned about catching the flu, you would go to your doctor and pay for a flu shot. Your decision to get a flu shot creates spillover benefits for the people around you. Your immunity reduces the chance that they will contract the disease even though they did not pay for it. Economists refer to these people as free riders.

When production of a good or service creates a positive externality, there is never enough of it. In order to increase the desirable good or service, government might choose to subsidize its production. Government subsidizes public schools for this reason. Even though private schools exist, there are not enough private schools to educate the population. An educated population creates a positive externality, so government subsidizes education for all children. Businesses in America do not have to teach their workers to read the employee manual or compute math problems.

NEGATIVE EXTERNALITY

Negative externalities occur when the production or consumption of a good or service creates spillover costs to society. Pollution is an example of a negative externality of the production process. For example, a shoe manufacturer produces shoes, but it also produces air pollution that is released outside the factory. When the firm sells the shoes to its customers, the cost of the pollution is not factored into the price of the shoes. People living near the factory bear part of the cost of production in the form of pollution, but do not receive payment for the shoes that the factory makes. When a firm's production creates a negative externality, there is too much of the good being produced. In a situation like this, government can tax the producer to reduce the amount of shoes, and pollution, produced.

BLACK MARKETS

Despite the best efforts of government, whenever and wherever government attempts to control prices or meddle with the forces of supply and demand, you can be sure a black market (illegal trade) will develop. Markets develop when there is a supply of and a demand for a product. It does not matter what it is. If someone makes it and people want it, there is a market for it. Furthermore, if government intervention creates surpluses or shortages, some enterprising individual will step in and provide a means of circumventing government and clearing the market, ensuring that supply matches up perfectly with demand.

Thwarting Price Ceilings

When government establishes a maximum price, shortages result for the good or service. This shortage is remedied by the market. In New York City, a system of rent controls dating back to World War II is still in place. As a result, very desirable apartments can be rented at extremely low prices. But at the low prices, very few apartments are available. People with significant income might be willing to rent some of these apartments, but are unable to do so legally. The market has responded with black market subletting. A renter benefiting from the rent control will turn around and sublet the apartment to a renter willing to pay a much higher rent (which is still lower than average). Recall that voluntary trade is wealth creating, so both the new renter and the original renter benefit from the transaction. In addition, the landlord is no worse off than before the sublet occurred. Yet the city of New York actively pursues these illegal sublets. Every year, the city uses scarce resources to enforce this system of price controls. A solution would be to remove the rent controls and allow the market to determine the price of rent.

Rent Controls

As of 2024 only two states, California and Oregon, have statewide rent controls in place. Other areas, such as Washington DC and New York City, also have some level of rent control in place. Under these systems, landlords can only increase rent for existing tenants by specific amounts, usually 10% or less.

Sporting events also provide an example of the inefficient outcome created by price controls. Who wants to see an event more, someone willing to pay $50 or someone willing to pay $1,000? When ticket prices are limited, those willing to pay more are forced to compete with those who would actually receive less utility from seeing the event.

Thwarting Price Floors

Markets also develop to thwart price floors. Workers willing to work for less than minimum wage might resort to contract labor or receiving illegal cash payments. Situations where workers are forced to accept low wages or face deportation are not mutually beneficial, nor are they voluntary. Exploitation occurs when one party to a transaction is unable to freely choose whether or not to engage in the transaction. Assuming that the transaction is voluntary, both business and workers benefit. If the transaction were not mutually beneficial, then it would not occur.

FINANCIAL MARKETS AND LOANABLE FUNDS THEORY

What's Behind the Curtain?

Have you ever wondered what the people on the news are talking about when they say something like, "The Dow Jones Industrial Average closed up 30 points today on heavy trading. The S&P 500 also edged higher. The Nasdaq was mixed. Foreign markets opened lower on news that the Fed will maintain near-zero interest rates for the foreseeable future. Corporate bond prices sank as many issues were downgraded while the yield on the ten-year Treasury ended lower"?

If you subscribe to *The Wall Street Journal* or *Financial Times*, or regularly watch CNBC, Bloomberg, or the Fox Business channel, you probably understand the lingo. But if you're like many Americans, the financial markets are a complete mystery. Even though they appear complicated, financial markets serve a very basic purpose: to connect the people who have money with the people who want money.

LOANABLE FUNDS THEORY

Economists offer a simple model for understanding financial markets and how the real interest rate is determined. (Remember that the real interest rate is the amount of nominal interest left standing after the rate of inflation is accounted for/subtracted.) Like many bright ideas economists come up with, this model is purely imaginary but it helps to explain what happens in financial markets. The hypothetical market they've identified is referred to as the loanable funds market. It exists to bring together "savers" and "borrowers." Savers supply and borrowers demand. The real interest rate occurs at the point where the amount saved equals the amount borrowed.

According to the law of supply, producers are only willing to offer more if they can collect a higher price because they face ever-increasing costs. In the loanable funds market, the price is the real interest rate. Savers, the producers of loanable funds, respond to the price by offering more funds as the rate increases and less as the rate decreases. Borrowers act as consumers of loanable funds—their behavior is explained by the law of demand. When the interest rate is high, they are less willing and able to borrow, and when interest rates are low, they are more willing and able to borrow.

Money Talks

investment

In economics, investment means borrowing in order to purchase physical capital. If the topic is stocks and bonds, then investment is understood to mean pretty much the same thing as saving. Savers engage in financial investment, which provides the funds for borrowers to engage in capital investment.

According to the expanded view of the loanable funds theory, savers are represented by households, businesses, governments, and the foreign sector. Borrowers also are represented by these same sectors. Changes in the saving and borrowing behavior of the various sectors of the economy result in change in the real interest rate and change in the quantity of loanable funds exchanged. For example, a decision by foreign savers to save more in the United States results in a lower real interest rate and a greater quantity of loanable funds exchanged for the country. A decision by the US government to borrow money and engage in deficit spending would increase the demand for loanable funds and result in a higher real interest rate. This encourages more savings, leading to a greater quantity of loanable funds exchanged. The loanable funds theory of interest rate determination is useful for understanding changes in long-term interest rates.

LIQUIDITY PREFERENCE

John Maynard Keynes's liquidity preference theory explains short-term nominal interest rates. Instead of looking at saving and borrowing behavior as the determinant of interest rates, Keynes taught that short-term interest rates are a function of consumers' liquidity preference or inclination for holding cash. In Keynes's theory, the money market, as opposed to the loanable funds market, was central to explaining interest rates.

The money market is where the central bank supplies money, and households, businesses, and government demand money at various nominal interest rates. Central banks like America's Federal Reserve act as regulated monopolies and issue money independent of the interest rate. Liquidity preference is the demand for money. At high nominal interest rates, people would rather hold interest-bearing non-cash assets like bonds, but as interest rates fall, people are more willing to hold cash as an asset because they are not sacrificing much interest to do so.

Economic Theories Compete Too

Why are there two theories of interest rate determination? Economists have competing theories for many economic phenomena. Interest rates are just one of many concepts on which economists have differing points of view. The loanable funds theory is associated with classical economics, whereas the money market theory is associated with Keynesian economics.

If the Fed wants to lower the nominal interest rate to encourage investment and consumption, they increase the money supply, and if they wish to raise nominal interest rates in order to curtail investment and consumption, they decrease the available supply of money. Increases or decreases in the nominal gross domestic product cause the demand for money to either increase or decrease.

Assuming that the Fed holds the supply of money constant, increases in money demand result in a higher nominal interest rate, whereas decreases in money demand reduce the nominal interest rate.

THE MONEY MARKET

I'll Have a T-Bill with a Side of Fries

As previously described, the money market is where the central bank supplies money, and households, businesses, and government demand money at various nominal interest rates. Firms, banks, and governments are able to obtain short-term financing in the money market. Securities (financial instruments such as stocks and bonds) with maturities of less than one year are included in this market.

COMMERCIAL PAPER

Businesses with excellent credit can easily borrow in the money market by issuing commercial paper, which is nothing more than a short-term IOU. For example, Behemoth Corporation is expecting payments from its customers at the end of the month, but has to pay its employees before then. In this case, Behemoth Corporation can issue commercial paper in exchange for cash to pay its employees. As soon as the customers make their payments to Behemoth Corporation, the company can turn around and repay whoever holds its commercial paper. For the company, commercial paper allows them to manage their cash flow at a cheaper rate than taking on longer-term debt would allow, and for the lender it provides a liquid and relatively safe way to earn some interest on their extra cash.

Commercial paper is an unsecured debt, meaning that it doesn't represent any type of ownership interest and no collateral is offered in exchange. You're repaid by cash flow (as in the example just presented, once the customers pay Behemoth Corporation at the end of the month, you'll get your original investment plus interest back). If the firm defaults on their repayment, you're stuck without a lot of good options. It's not as if you can send out the neighborhood repo guy and seize the office furniture.

Companies with less-than-perfect credit have to offer higher interest rates in order to get any takers, who will be assuming more than the usual risk. Demand is much greater for higher-rated commercial paper. Commercial paper is usually sold in big chunks (say, $100,000 per issue), the interest is taxable, and the Securities and Exchange Commission (SEC) doesn't regulate their sale. This is why money market funds are popular with private investors (the little guys like you and me). They allow for diversification, spreading the risk out over a number of different commercial paper investments.

TREASURY BILLS

Like corporations, sometimes the US government needs a little cash on hand to make the wheels of governance run smoothly. When it does, it auctions Treasury bills (T-bills) for its short-term cash needs. The T-bills have various maturities of less than one year. Investors like T-bills because they allow them to earn risk-free interest while maintaining liquidity in case they need their cash quickly for other purposes. The government benefits because T-bills provide the government with easy access to cash for government spending, and what government doesn't love easy access to cash?

How Discounting Works

T-bills are different from other forms of government securities in that they are sold at a discount from face value. T-bills have a face value of $1,000, but buyers pay less than that. The difference between the face value and the amount paid represents an interest payment. For example, if Rich Personne buys a 52-week $1,000 T-bill for $950, he will receive interest of $50 at maturity, which is equivalent to earning 5.26% on a $950 investment.

FEDERAL FUNDS

Banks, like any other business, sometimes have to have access to more cash than they have tucked away in the vault. To meet their short-term financing needs, they lend and borrow federal funds, also known as fed funds. Banks may borrow from each other in the fed funds market to satisfy their legal reserve requirements or to meet their clearing balance requirements (the amount needed to settle all of a day's transactions). This component of the money market is important for maintaining bank liquidity. It also increases efficiency by encouraging banks to put all of their available excess reserves to work earning a return. Because banks keep most of their reserves on deposit with the Fed, the exchange of these federal funds occurs almost immediately as the banks exchange their reserve balances between each other. The Federal Reserve affects this market by influencing the fed funds rate, which is the interest rate banks charge each other for the use of overnight federal funds.

THE BOND MARKET

Call Me Bond, Coupon Bond

For long-term financing, governments and firms are able to borrow in the bond market. When investors buy bonds, they are lending money to sellers with the expectation that they will be repaid their principal plus interest. For bond issuers, the bond market provides an efficient means of borrowing large sums of money. For the buyer, bonds provide a relatively secure financial investment that provides interest income.

FEDERAL GOVERNMENT BONDS

You are probably familiar with two types of bonds: coupon bonds and zero-coupon bonds. Coupon bonds are sold at or near face value and provide guaranteed interest payments. Zero-coupon bonds are sold at a discount from face value and pay face value at maturity.

Either type makes an attractive investment for people seeking interest income while preserving their principal. The ability to sell bonds on the secondary market makes them relatively liquid, which is also important to investors.

The US government issues several types of bonds with maturities greater than a year. Treasury notes and Treasury bonds are primary sources for financing the federal budget. Treasury notes are medium-term securities with maturities ranging from two to ten years. Treasury bonds are long-term securities that mature after twenty to thirty years.

The interest rate on the ten-year Treasury note is important because it serves as a benchmark interest rate for both corporate bonds and mortgages. As the interest rate on the ten-year Treasury note fluctuates, corporate rates and mortgage rates fluctuate as well.

In addition to the Treasury, independent agencies of the US government are able to borrow by issuing bonds. Although they lack the guarantee of repayment that Treasury securities have, agency securities are backed by the government and as such are seen as virtually guaranteed. The Federal National Mortgage Association (Fannie Mae), the Federal Home Loan Mortgage Corporation (Freddie Mac), and the Student Loan Marketing Association (Sallie Mae) are well-known agencies that issue bonds in order to finance their operations. Agency securities provide an alternative for investors looking for the security of government bonds but with higher interest rates.

STATE AND LOCAL GOVERNMENT BONDS

State and local governments are also able to borrow through the bond market. Municipal bonds often finance schools, roads, and other public projects. The interest paid on the municipal bonds is exempt from federal income taxes, which makes them attractive to investors. Because the interest is tax exempt, municipal bonds do not have to offer as high an interest rate to attract investors. As a result, state and local governments are able to borrow more cheaply than the private sector.

CORPORATE BONDS

Firms are able to borrow in the bond market by issuing corporate bonds. Corporate bonds provide businesses with the money they need for capital investment without having to arrange bank financing. In addition, corporate bonds allow for businesses to obtain funds without diluting ownership in the company. The chief advantage of bonds is that they provide firms with financial leverage. For example, if a company has $1,000 to invest in capital and can expect a return of 10%, the company will earn $100 from the investment. If, however, the firm borrows $1,000,000 and invests in capital that returns 10% a year, the firm is able to earn $100,000 without risking its own money. Because firms lack the ability to tax to repay bonds (and therefore occasionally default on them), investors require a higher interest rate on corporate bonds than on Treasury and municipal bonds to offset the increased risk.

BOND RISKS

Bonds are not without their downsides. Investors face investment risk, inflation risk, interest rate risk, and the risk of early call (early call means the issuer can recall ["retire"] the bond before the expected maturity date).

- Governments or firms *may* fail to pay back their borrowed money, so all bondholders face investment risk.
- If the rate of inflation increases during the life of a bond, the investor's return is offset by the inflation.

- If interest rates increase during the life of a bond, the value of the bond decreases until its effective yield equals the new higher interest rate. For bondholders, this means that they might lose principal if they try to sell it before maturity.
- If interest rates decline during the life of a bond, the issuer may find it beneficial to retire or recall the old bonds and refinance at the new lower interest rate. For bondholders, this means that they lose out on earning the higher interest they would have had when the bond matured.

Prospective investors rely on rating agencies to determine the quality of the bonds. Moody's, Standard & Poor's, and Fitch rate bonds from "investment grade" to "junk" to "in default." Bonds with lower ratings must reward the investor with a higher interest rate to compensate for the additional risk that interest and principal payments will not be made.

Historically, US government bonds had the highest possible rating from all three agencies as they were considered "no-risk" investments. However, in August 2023, Fitch downgraded the ratings of long-term Treasury bonds due to concerns over an increasing debt burden, budget stand-offs in Congress, and "expected fiscal deterioration over the next three years."

INTEREST RATES REVISITED

Interest rates are made up of several components: the real rate, expected inflation premium, default risk premium, liquidity premium, and maturity risk. The real rate and the expected inflation premium make up the risk-free rate of return. This risk-free rate of return acts as the benchmark on which all other interest rates are based. Historically, the various bonds issued by the US Treasury acted as the proxies for the risk-free rate of return; that changed in August 2023.

Treasury securities are considered reliable instruments because the United States has never defaulted on its debt in its 240-plus-year history, and the secondary market for US Treasury securities is considered "deep" because it is backed by the full faith and credit of the United States. The importance of the secondary market in the Treasury cannot be understated. Because so many governments, banks, businesses, and individuals desire US Treasury securities as a low-risk place to park their money, a condition is created where there is little doubt to the liquidity of the securities. The main risk faced by the holders of Treasury securities is maturity risk. The longer the term of a bond, the greater the chance that interest rates will change from the one that existed at the time of purchase. If interest rates were to unexpectedly rise during the life of the bond, the value of the bond would decrease. As new bond prices fall, the effective interest rate on the bonds increase, which makes previously issued bonds less attractive. This, in turn, makes them less valuable.

Money Talks

maturity risk
The risk that a bond's value will be negatively impacted by changes in interest rates. That risk increases with longer maturities (bond due dates).

THE STOCK MARKET

Taking Stock of Companies

Of all the financial markets, none receives as much media coverage as the stock market. Unlike bond markets, where investors are making loans to governments and firms, the stock market is where investors are able to purchase partial ownership in firms represented by shares of stock.

STOCKS SIMPLIFIED

For companies that want or need outside investment, issuing stock in an initial public offering (IPO) can be a good way to raise funds. Investors purchase the stock with the expectation that it will either pay dividends or earn capital gains through price increases. Investors earn dividends when a company divides a portion of the profits among all of the owners according to the number of shares each owns. For example, if a company has 100 shares of stock, earns profits of $1,000,000, and decides to distribute half of the profits to its shareholders, each share will earn a dividend of $500,000/100 or $5,000.

Stocks earn capital gains when they're sold at a higher price than their cost when purchased. Suppose you buy a share of General Motors (GM) for $35.75, and a few months later GM announces a hot new car that runs on sunlight rather than gasoline. Demand drives the price of the stock higher. When it reaches $50.25, you decide to sell and realize a capital gain of $14.50.

The majority of stock purchases and sales occur in the secondary market. When you place an order to buy stock, you are most likely buying shares that were previously owned by another individual. If Tina buys Coca-Cola stock in the market, she is buying it from someone else, not Coca-Cola. The only time the firm receives money in a stock purchase is through an IPO or when the firm sells stock that it had repurchased earlier.

BULLS AND BEARS

Stock market activity is often described as "bull" or "bear." Bull markets see a lot of trading activity and increasing stock prices, while bear markets see somewhat depressed activity—mainly selloffs—and declining stock values. Which characterization applies depends mainly on the prevailing direction of stock prices, but that is not the only factor in play. Other issues that contribute to bull and bear markets may include investor emotions, economic ups and downs, supply and demand, and global conditions. Investors, and the stock market itself, are heavily influenced by economic indicators like unemployment rates and GDP announcements. Conversely, the stock market—or at least portions of it—can act as an economic indicator. Bull markets tend to correlate with thriving economies, high employment, and growing GDP. Bear markets go along with flailing economies, higher unemployment, and stale GDP.

THE RISE OF FUNDS

For a long time, the stock market was a playground for the rich, people who were able to afford to buy blocks of shares in many different companies. The average American didn't have enough free cash flow or income to play there, and were largely excluded from this potential path toward wealth. Then mutual funds hit the scene in 1924, and everything began to change.

Mutual funds are single investments that hold hundreds (even thousands) of other investments. Having a single share of a mutual fund gives investors access to all of the stocks (or other securities) owned by the fund. They effectively pool the cash of many investors to create a well-balanced, comprehensive portfolio. Suddenly, everyone can afford to invest in the stock market, and mutual funds began to greatly influence the direction of the market as shares were bought and sold. This also had the effect of bringing more cash into the capital markets, funding more business creation and growth to broaden the economy.

Decades later, in the 1990s, exchange traded funds (ETFs) entered the scene. Unlike mutual funds whose shares have to be bought and sold directly from the fund itself, ETFs trade like stocks over the stock exchange, giving investors more freedom and flexibility with their fund investing. This growing sector of the financial industry has injected billions of dollars into the markets, improving investor liquidity and increasing investor cash flows to emerging and developing nations.

SO WHAT'S THE POINT?

Ultimately the function of these various markets is to allow savers to connect with borrowers. Businesses seeking to expand their capital investment look to the stock market as a source of needed funds.

Interest Rate and Investment

There is an inverse relationship between the interest rate and investment. The lower the interest rate, the lower the cost of capital, and the more firms are able to invest in physical capital. Likewise, as the interest rate increases, the cost of capital increases, and firms become less willing to borrow to invest in physical capital.

Raising money through equity (issuing stocks) can be cheaper than increasing debt, but it does dilute ownership and control over the company. Judicious use of equity financing raises enough capital for investment and growth without giving up full control of the company. On the economic scale, this provides funding for everything from expanded facilities to additional investment in human capital to increased shareholder dividends, all of which can feed into a more robust economy.

FOREIGN EXCHANGE AND FOREIGN TRADE

C'est La Vie, No Es?

Whether you know it or not, foreign exchange is a part of your everyday life. From the products you buy to the vacations you take, foreign exchange affects much of what you do. The flow of currency between nations is also a matter of recordkeeping. The balance of payments records all of the inflows and outflows of currency from a country. The sum of net exports, net foreign factor income, and net transfers is the current account balance, while net foreign investment and official reserves make up the financial account. That all starts with exchange rates.

EXCHANGE RATES

Whenever one currency is exchanged for another, foreign exchange has occurred and an exchange rate has been paid. The exchange rate is nothing more than the current price of a currency in terms of another currency. For example, $1 may buy you €0.92, £0.79, ¥148.28, or S_{Fr} 0.88.

Exchange rates are determined in the world's largest market, the foreign exchange market. Annual trade volume approaches $2.4 quadrillion (a thousand trillion), with transactions occurring twenty-four hours a day. The foreign exchange market is dominated by the British, Americans, and Japanese with the vast majority of trades occurring in the US dollar. The euro (€), pound sterling (£),

Japanese yen (¥), and Swiss franc (S$_{Fr}$) are the other hard currencies most often traded.

Who's Involved?

Large banks are the main players in the foreign exchange market, brought together through a system of interconnected brokers. The banks serve both corporate and individual customers who need foreign exchange in order to conduct business. Central banks also participate in the foreign exchange market in order to either manipulate exchange rates or to correct imbalances between their country's current and financial accounts.

As consumers' tastes for imported goods change, so does the exchange rate between the countries involved. The popularity of cars and consumer electronics from South Korea among American consumers necessarily creates a demand for South Korea's currency, the won (₩).

Interest Rates and Inflation

Changes in real interest rates also affect the foreign exchange market. Changing interest rates can cause sudden fluctuations in exchange rates. When one country's real interest rate rises relative to another country, savings flow toward the higher interest rate. With all other things equal, increases in American interest rates relative to Japanese interest rates will cause an increased supply of yen and increased demand for dollars as Japanese savers seek to earn higher American interest rates. The result is an appreciated dollar and depreciated yen. Eventually, the dollar's appreciation relative to the yen will offset any gains made off of the interest rate difference. This is referred to as interest rate parity.

Inflation in an economy provides an incentive for its people to exchange their currency for one that is more stable. The result of inflation is to not only reduce the value of the currency domestically but also in foreign exchange.

Probably the most counterintuitive outcome results from differences in economic rates of growth. As an economy's income increases relative to another country, the exchange rate between the two changes. For example, if Canada's income increases relative to the United States' income, the Canadian dollar weakens relative to the US dollar. Why? As Canadians experience higher incomes, their propensity to import also increases. In other words, as you get richer, you go shopping more often and supply more currency in foreign exchange. The counterintuitive outcome is that as an economy strengthens, its currency weakens, and as an economy weakens, its currency strengthens.

EXPORTS AND THE BALANCE OF TRADE

In the United States, most producers focus on meeting the demands of the domestic market. Some, however, produce goods and services for export to foreign markets. Other businesses import those goods and services for which there is a demand or the United States does not produce. More than 40% of the United States' trade occurs with Canada, Mexico, and China.

THE BALANCE OF TRADE

Net exports, or the balance of trade, is equal to the value of all exports minus the value of all imports. Net exports in the United States are negative because the value of imports exceeds the value of exports. This is referred to as a balance of trade deficit. Other countries like China, Germany, and Ireland have balance of trade surpluses because the value of their exports exceeds that of their imports.

The balance of trade can be further broken down into the balance of trade in goods and the balance of trade in services. For the United States, the balance of trade in goods is what contributes to the trade deficit. Americans prefer foreign consumer goods and resources. On the other hand, the United States tends to be a net exporter of services. America's logistical know-how as well as its engineering, legal, and other technical services are exported to the rest of the world.

The Bureau of Economic Analysis

The Commerce Department's Bureau of Economic Analysis (BEA) is the government agency responsible for measuring the balance of trade. According to the BEA, as of November 2023, the trade deficit measured approximately $63.2 billion. This total trade deficit was composed of a $253.7-billion trade in exported goods and services combined with a $316.9 billion trade in imported goods and services.

OFFICIAL RESERVES AND EXCHANGE RATE POLICY

Central banks, like the US Federal Reserve System, maintain reserves of foreign currency or official reserves. The purpose of official reserves is to provide a stabilizing influence in the foreign exchange market. If a balance of payments deficit occurs, the Federal Reserve reduces its foreign reserves in order to zero out the balance. In the case of a balance of payments surplus, the Federal Reserve acquires additional foreign reserves to zero out the balance.

The United States is in the unique position of issuing the reserve currency for the majority of countries as most countries' foreign reserve holdings are in US dollars. The size of China's and Japan's official reserves has been a cause of concern for many in the financial community. As of 2023, these Asian countries have over $4 trillion worth of reserves in US dollars. Some economists and financial experts fear that if China or Japan were to reduce their dollar holdings, a collapse could ensue from a sudden increase in the supply of dollars in foreign exchange.

To Fix or Float? That Is the Question

At the end of World War II, countries met in Bretton Woods, New Hampshire and established a fixed exchange rate system pegged to the dollar. That allowed businesses to easily engage in foreign trade without fear of losing money from fluctuating exchange rates. In addition, by pegging currencies to the stable dollar, foreign governments were responsible for practicing sound economic policies such as not creating inflation by recklessly printing currency. At first this was very successful, but by 1971 it had completely collapsed.

Today, many approaches to exchange rates exist. Some countries let their currency float, others peg their currency to the dollar, and still others have unified under a single currency. The United States and United Kingdom allow their respective currencies to float on the foreign exchange market, which means that they do not use official reserves to maintain exchange rates. That lets policymakers use interest rate policies to encourage domestic growth or slow inflation without having to consider exchange rates.

Hong Kong, for example, pegs their currency to the US dollar by actively trading their holdings of foreign reserves. This allows their respective currencies to maintain a competitive advantage against others in the American market.

The turn of this century saw another approach to exchange rate policy. Europe unified its economy under a single currency, the euro. France and Germany, for example, can now trade freely without regard to exchange rates. The advent of the euro created the world's second largest currency after the dollar.

Money Talks

monetary policy
Efforts by the central bank of a country to stabilize prices, promote full employment, and encourage long-run economic growth through controlling the money supply and interest rates.

CRYPTOCURRENCY

The Magic of Digital Money

Cryptocurrency has the word "currency" right in its name, but it's not considered legal tender, at least not in the US. That doesn't mean people don't use it like money. Many major platforms, like PayPal and Shopify, now accept certain crypto coins as payment for goods and services, with more sure to join the party.

These currencies can be either traded like stocks or spent like money, and their asset status (whether they're money or securities) remains unclear.

THE CRYPTO REVOLUTION

Cryptocurrency, as we know it now, first came on the scene quietly when Bitcoin was released as open-source code. The new peer-to-peer currency was launched by the mysterious Satoshi Nakamoto, a pseudonym still surrounded by secrecy and conjecture, in a paper that revealed groundbreaking blockchain technology. The first bitcoins were mined by people solving complex math problems correctly to verify their transactions, resulting in a small amount of bitcoin in their wallets.

Since then, crypto has exploded. Now more than 23,000 cryptocurrencies with a combined market value of over $1 trillion trade regularly, though most of them are relative unknowns. The biggest names in cryptocurrency include:

- Bitcoin
- Ethereum

- Dogecoin
- Cardano
- Litecoin
- Tether
- Binance
- XRP

New cryptocurrencies pop up virtually every day, as they are easy to create and market.

Now You Don't See It

Crypto coins and tokens have no physical form. They're not stored somewhere. Rather, they're scattered bits of data floating in a massive database that only the owner can gather up and access.

Powered by Blockchain

Blockchain is a digital record book, or ledger, with no central server home. The information is decentralized and widely distributed throughout a large peer-to-peer network to record data in blocks. Each block is stored on many servers, and they must all match exactly for the block to remain valid. With this set up, no block can be changed after the fact—they're irreversible and tamper-proof. Transactions can be confirmed without having to pass through a central clearing authority, like a bank.

Crypto Wallets

Owning and using cryptocurrencies calls for a digital wallet. These pieces of software can live on a phone, tablet, or laptop, or exist in the cloud. They hold encryption keys that confirm the user's identity, directly link to their cryptocurrencies, and allow crypto-based transactions to take place.

Every wallet has public and private keys. The public key identifies a specific wallet address. Private keys can access and manage the coins linked to the wallet. If private keys are lost, so are the cryptocurrencies held in the wallet.

There are two main types of crypto wallets: custodial and noncustodial. Custodial wallets exist on third-party platforms, like cryptocurrency exchanges, where they hold wallets for users. Noncustodial wallets are held by the users themselves, who have total responsibility for the associated keys. Most crypto owners use noncustodial wallets.

CRYPTOCURRENCY AND THE ECONOMY

Legal tender, what we think of as money, is backed by governments. It has a set value for exchange that (for the most part) remains relatively steady: a dollar is worth a dollar every day. It can be used legally to settle debts, pay taxes, and buy goods and services; the person, business, or government agency being paid must accept legal tender.

Cryptocurrency is not considered legal tender in most of the world, though it seems to be gaining ground. So far, only El Salvador and the Central African Republic recognize Bitcoin (but not all cryptocurrencies) as legal tender. While most countries allow cryptocurrency to exist legally, some countries (including China and Egypt) have outlawed or restricted its use.

From an economic perspective, cryptocurrencies offer some benefits over legal tender. Transactions can be completed in seconds rather than taking days to clear. Crypto transactions also tend to be less expensive to process (think credit card fees and wire transfer fees, for example). In areas where many people don't have access to traditional banking, crypto makes trading easier to manage.

Wild Swings in Value

Unlike legal tender, cryptocurrency values fluctuate wildly and often. That's because their value is influenced by a variety of factors including:

- Supply and demand
- Social media hype
- Government interventions
- Investor emotions
- Rumors
- Competition

Crypto prices can rise or fall by hundreds of dollars in a single day and fluctuate even more wildly over longer periods. Bitcoin, for example, went from nearly $20,000 in December 2017 to less than $3,500 just one year later. The price swung up to $65,000 in November 2021, then up and down over and over again until it hit $44,000 in December 2023 and $49,000 in January 2024.

That volatility makes cryptocurrency a risky store of value, one that can disappear overnight.

The Tax Effects

Since cryptocurrencies are considered investments in the US, many transactions are considered taxable where they wouldn't be if they were transacted with money. In fact, one of the few transactions that won't trigger taxes is buying crypto with fiat money. Taxable transactions include:

- Selling crypto
- Exchanging one type of coin for another type (like Bitcoin for Dogecoin)
- Paying someone for services with crypto
- Buying something with crypto

The Internal Revenue Service (IRS) treats these transactions as if you'd sold stock, and then used the proceeds. If you receive cryptocurrency as a form of payment for anything that would normally be taxable, such as wages, interest, or consulting fees, that also counts as taxable income to you.

The tax treatment can get tricky because it's based on the difference between the value of the cryptocurrency when you bought it and when you used, sold, or exchanged it. People that own cryptocurrency must track all their transactions meticulously for proper and complete tax reporting.

The Criminal Component

The cryptocurrency arena is fraught with fraud. Since it's an anonymous means of exchange that skips over regulated banking institutions, cryptocurrency is widely used by criminals around the world. The investment arena is also full of scams including nonexistent, fraudulent coins and overhyped new crypto projects that lure in investors, then disappear with their money.

ECONOMIC SECTORS

Just Goin' with the Flow

In an economic system, people's self-interest is manifested in markets and through the political process. Both are intertwined and affect each other; an economist would be unlikely to look at any part of the political process without considering how it affects markets. An economic model called the circular flow model shows the relationship between households, firms, governments, and the foreign sector as they all interact in product (e.g., goods), factor (e.g., labor), and financial (e.g., stock, bond) markets. These markets are also interrelated, as you no doubt have concluded from the previous discussions of them, but this theory helps show and describe this interrelationship.

THE PRIVATE SECTOR

The starting point for understanding the entire economy is a very simple model that illustrates how households and firms interact in the product market and the factor market. The private sector is nothing more than the households and businesses in an economy. Households buy goods and services from firms in the product market with money they earned by selling their labor and entrepreneurship to the firms (via the factor market) in exchange for wages and profits. Households also sell natural resources to the firms in exchange for rents.

Firms employ land, labor, capital, and entrepreneurship in order to provide goods and services.

Factor Flow and Market Flow

There are two sets of flows between households and firms. Flowing in one direction are goods and services in the product market, and land, labor, capital, and entrepreneurship in the factor market. Consumption spending flows in the opposite direction of the goods and services. Flowing opposite the factors of production are factor payments, which include rent, wages, interest, and profits.

THE PUBLIC SECTOR

The public sector refers to all levels of government, from local to federal. The public sector interacts with households by purchasing some of the factors of production (such as land or labor) in exchange for the factor payments (such as wage, rent, or interest). Government also interacts with firms by buying goods and services in the product market.

Government combines the factors of production with the goods and services it buys from firms in order to provide public goods and services to the private sector. National defense, police, fire protection, schools, libraries, and roads are examples of the types of public goods and services provided by the public sector.

Taxes, in both the factor market and the product market, are the source of governments' income. Sometimes the government subsidizes firms with tax breaks or direct payments and households with payments like unemployment, disability, or stimulus payments. These are examples of a flow of money from government to firms or individuals.

THE FOREIGN SECTOR

The United States' economy does not exist in isolation; it's part of the much larger world economy. The foreign sector refers to the rest of the world.

The US economy interacts with the rest of the world in the product, factor, and financial markets. The circular flow theory accounts for the interaction of markets throughout this larger world economy, not just domestically.

In the product market, some of the domestically produced goods and services are exported to people in other countries. In the same manner, not all of the goods and services that are purchased by households and government are domestically produced. Americans import goods and services from the rest of the world.

Americans also trade the factors of production with the rest of the world. Land, labor, capital, and entrepreneurship flow from the rest of the world in exchange for foreign factor payments. Also, the factors of production flow to the rest of the world in exchange for foreign factor income. If a US citizen earns income abroad, that is foreign factor income. Payments to foreigners for the use of the factors of production incur a foreign factor payment.

Foreign Transfers

A considerable amount of money is transferred to other countries not in payment for goods and services but to help support family members. This type of transfer, called a remittance, affects the economy but does not constitute a direct exchange in a market. India is a prime example of a country dependent upon a large expatriate community. Many Indians living abroad remit money to their extended families back in India.

Foreign Investment

The goal of foreign investment is to earn foreign factor income in the form of interest and profits. A decision by American entrepreneurs to buy land and develop a theme park in Iceland, although not the best idea, would create an inflow of dollars to Iceland with the purpose of creating an outflow of kronur to America as foreign factor income.

Foreign investment can also be used to finance a trade deficit, as is the case with the United States. Currently, the United States is able to enjoy cheap Chinese imports in excess of US exports to China because of a counterbalancing flow of savings from China to the United States. For every dollar spent on Chinese imports, there is a return flow as the Chinese use the same dollars to purchase both American exports and also American financial assets.

THE FINANCIAL SECTOR AND FINANCIAL MARKETS

The financial sector includes intermediaries like banks, credit unions, insurance companies, and stock exchanges that help to facilitate all of the transactions that have been mentioned. Their importance cannot be underestimated as they stand in the middle of almost all transactions. Without them, most modern markets would be unable to function.

Financial Intermediaries

Transactions conducted in the product market typically involve the use of debit cards, credit cards, apps like Apple Pay, cash drawn from ATMs, or, in the case of exports and imports, foreign exchange. All of these services are provided by the financial intermediaries for a fee.

This is all about making it easy for people to spend money and it's in the background of everything, including buying or selling stock, trading dollars for euros before you go to Paris, opening a doggie daycare and looking for start-up funding, or paying your electric bill through autopay.

Financial Intermediaries and the Factor Market

Financial intermediaries are equally involved in the factor market. This is not because they use land and labor (although they do). It is because they are involved in most transactions in the factor market. Most working Americans receive a paycheck, not cash. The paycheck gets deposited in a bank or credit union. Buying and selling land (a factor) almost always involves financial intermediaries. Capital itself is a factor of production. Where do people find capital? Yup. In the financial sector.

The Financial Sector and Savings

The financial sector generates a significant amount of revenue in the form of interest payments for mortgages and loans. That fact is connected to a dimension of the circular flow theory that we haven't discussed yet—the part of the economy that involves savings, not spending.

The Financial Markets

Up to this point, all of the income that has been earned by households, firms, government, and the rest of the world has been spent in the circular flow model. Dollar in = dollar out. But private, public, and foreign sectors don't only spend money—they also save it. To account for the fact that the different economic sectors save a portion of their income, the circular flow model enters the third dimension: the financial markets.

Households save for the future, government can run a budget surplus, businesses retain earnings for future investment, and the foreign sector engages in portfolio investment in the United States. Savings flow to financial intermediaries and from there (in the form of loans) to all sectors of the economy.

THE GROSS DOMESTIC PRODUCT

Keeping Score

Keeping score is important. If you are trying to lose a few extra pounds, stepping on the scale from time to time allows you to evaluate your performance. In school, teachers assign grades to assess students' level of understanding. In baseball, statistics on nearly every aspect of the game are used to determine the pitchers and the batting order. Data and statistics are useful for making informed decisions. During the 1930s, the US government wanted to better understand the economy's ability to generate the necessary materials for the war effort. This led to the development of gross domestic product (GDP) by American economist Simon Kuznets as a means of measuring economic output. GDP is important today as an overall indicator of economic performance.

WEALTH AND INCOME

GDP measures the total value of all final production that occurs within a country during the course of a year. GDP is also a measure of annual spending on new domestic production and a measure of income earned from domestic production. To better understand GDP, consider the following example. Assume we have a simple economy made up of Frank and Dana. Lately Frank has been complaining about the cold weather, so he offers Dana $100 to knit a blanket. Dana jumps at the opportunity to make some money and commences knitting a new blanket. Upon completion, Dana exchanges the blanket for the $100. In this example, what was the value of the economy's spending, income, and output? The answer is $100. The $100 spent by Frank was earned by Dana in exchange for the knitted blanket. In 2022, US GDP was $25.46 trillion, because considerably more than one knitted blanket was produced.

GDP versus GNP

GNP, or gross national product, is also a measure of economic performance. The key difference between GDP and GNP is a single preposition. GDP is a measure of all new production that is done in a country during the year, while GNP is a measure of all new production that is done by a country during the year. Toyotas made in Texas are part of US GDP, but not US GNP.

GDP is not static. Instead, GDP is a flow. Imagine a bathtub with a running faucet and open drain. The water flowing from the faucet is GDP, the water accumulating in the tub is the wealth of the nation, and the water exiting the drain represents an outflow like depreciation. As long as the GDP exceeds outflows of wealth, the wealth of the nation grows. Essentially, GDP measures production that is new and is not a measure of accumulated wealth.

A LOOK BACK AT CIRCULAR FLOW

In the circular flow model, the economy has three primary sectors: private, public, and foreign. The private sector is further divided into households and businesses. Each sector contributes to the GDP. Households provide the factors of production that businesses use to produce goods and services. In addition, government provides the public goods not provided by the private sector. Furthermore, the foreign sector acts as a source of the factors of production as well as a source for goods and services. The foreign sector also functions as a market for domestic production.

GDP is represented in three ways in the circular flow model. The goods and services that businesses and government provide represent the value of all domestic production. The spending that the private, public, and foreign sector adds to the circular flow represents total spending. Finally, the rent, wages, interest, and profits earned in the factor market are a nation's income.

COUNTED OR NOT?

GDP includes much economic activity but not all of it. As a measure of production, GDP does not include purely financial transactions. When you purchase shares in the stock market, only the broker's commission would be counted in GDP. This is because the purchase of stock represents a transfer of ownership from one shareholder to another, and neither a good nor service is produced. Similarly, transfer payments like Social Security are not computed in GDP. Social Security payments are not made in return for the production of a new good or service, but instead represent a transfer from a taxed wage earner to a recipient.

Production for which no financial transaction occurs is also excluded from GDP. A stay-at-home parent who cares for the children, cleans the house, cooks, and runs errands certainly produces something of great value, but because no monetary payment is made, the value is undetermined and excluded. Interestingly, paying someone to do all of those activities would be included in GDP. Building a deck on your house, mowing your own grass, and changing your own oil are all services that can be purchased, but when you perform them for yourself, they are not included in GDP.

Apartment and house rent is included in consumption, and therefore GDP. Homeowners and mortgage payers do not pay rent, so the BEA imputes a rental payment on their housing. Whether you are an owner or a renter, when it comes to GDP, everyone is a renter.

To avoid overstating GDP, resale and intermediate production is excluded. Most home purchases are not counted in GDP. The resale of homes does not represent new production and is excluded. The only time home purchases are included is when the house is newly constructed. The primary reason resale is not counted is to avoid double-counting. Older homes were included in a previous year's GDP. Consider the sale of flour, butter, and sugar to a bakery that produces fresh bread. If the purchase of ingredients were included in GDP along with the sale of the fresh bread, the GDP would be overstated. To avoid this, GDP includes only final production of the bread. The price of the bread includes the earlier cost incurred in acquiring the ingredients.

GDP: PRIVATE SPENDING AND INVESTMENT

Because You're Worth It

GDP can be calculated by adding all of the expenditures on new domestic output. Households, businesses, governments, and other nations all spend money in the economy and each is represented in GDP by a different spending variable. Each type of expenditure is subject to various influences, and each can reveal important information about economic activity.

PERSONAL CONSUMPTION EXPENDITURE

Households engage in personal consumption expenditure. Personal consumption expenditure, or simply consumption, is the act of purchasing goods and services. More than two-thirds of all US GDP expenditures fall under the heading of consumption.

The ability of households to consume is chiefly constrained by disposable income, which is income after paying taxes. This fact gives government considerable leverage over households' capacity to consume. When it comes to available disposable income, consumers choose to either spend it in the product market or save it in the financial markets. This means that increased consumption results in less saving, and increased saving leads to decreased consumption.

Disposable Income Variables

Consumption is also sensitive to changes in consumers' wealth, interest rates, and expectations of the future. Increases in consumers' wealth tend to encourage consumption, while decreases tend to discourage it. The recent explosion of housing prices has had a positive effect on consumers' wealth. As a result, consumption and saving have increased because consumers are attempting to protect their net worth as they deal with rising prices. In addition to housing, much of consumers' wealth is in the form of retirement accounts. Therefore, changes in the stock market's key indicators like the Dow Jones Industrial Average and the S&P 500 often indicate the direction of household wealth, and thus consumption.

Durable goods like cars, appliances, and furniture are often purchased using borrowed money. Interest rates are then part of the equation to consume durables. High interest rates discourage durable goods consumption, and lower interest rates tend to encourage the purchase of durable goods. Plans designed to encourage durable goods consumption include 0% financing, interest-free for three years, and no payments until the next year.

Expectations as a determinant of consumption are easily understood. When people fear the future, they tend to save and not make any major purchases. In contrast, people that are upbeat about the future are more inclined to shop and less inclined to save.

Autonomous Consumption

Economists recognize that some consumption is independent of disposable income and refer to this as autonomous consumption. During periods of recession, consumption of durable goods is curtailed while consumption of essentials like food, rent, clothing, and healthcare remains relatively unaffected. Do you remember what it was like in March 2020 when COVID-19 lockdowns started? What type of consumption occurred and what type did not? Consumption of necessities and nondurables continued unabated, but consumption of durable goods (partly due to supply chain issues) and discretionary spending came to a halt.

GROSS PRIVATE INVESTMENT

Households and businesses engage in another expenditure referred to as gross private investment.

- Gross private investment includes business purchases of capital and inventory, and household purchases of new homes. Gross private investment is further broken down into net investment and depreciation.
- Net investment is the purchase of new capital that expands the economy's productive capacity.
- Depreciation is investment spending to replace worn capital.

It is important to note what investment is not. When it comes to calculating GDP, investment is not the purchase of stocks and bonds. That is financial investment or saving. What is being considered here is real investment. However, this real investment in the economy is financed by the financial investment that occurs in financial markets.

Money Talks

real investment
Real investment is money used to purchase tangible durable goods, like machinery, equipment, and buildings (including homes).

Future Expectations

The level of investment in the economy is influenced by expectations of future business conditions and interest rates. Positive expectations tend to boost investment while negative expectations result in less investment. Businesses respond this way in order to have the right amount of productive capacity to meet the expected future demand for their products. Interest rates are also a major consideration in the decision to invest. As interest rates rise, the relative profitability of investment decreases. Decisions to invest compare the expected rate of return to the current interest rate. As long as the expected rate of return exceeds the interest rate, businesses will undertake investment with the expectation of profit. Increased interest rates have the effect of making fewer investments profitable.

Planned and Unplanned Investment

Investment is divided into planned and unplanned investment. During periods of economic "normalcy," businesses invest in capital and inventory in order to turn around and sell it at a profit. This planned investment assumes that business conditions will continue according to the producers' expectations. When unplanned investment occurs, it is a sign of bad things to come. Automobile dealers order inventory from the factories to sell to consumers. If inventory begins to accumulate, that means consumers are not buying. The dealers stop ordering and the factory stops production. If this halt in production is pervasive, mass unemployment and economic recession occurs.

GDP: GOVERNMENT SPENDING AND EXPORTS

Spend It If You Got It

The GDP isn't measured just by adding together private spending and investment by households and businesses in the domestic market. It is also affected by government spending and international trade.

GOVERNMENT SPENDING

Government spending includes federal, state, and local expenditures on capital, infrastructure, and employee compensation. Military expenditures, road construction, and teacher salaries are all included. Government spending is financed by taxation and borrowing. The opportunity cost of government spending is the forgone consumption and gross private investment that might have otherwise occurred (you might have spent that $500 on a nice new TV but you had to send it to Uncle Sam instead). Transfer payments (such as Social Security benefits and certain subsidies to businesses) are not included as government spending for the purpose of calculating GDP.

Government spending accounts for about 40% of the GDP in the United States. Government spending as a percentage of GDP varies widely throughout the world, from a low of about 5.7% in countries such as Bangladesh and Ghana to about 57% in countries such as the Marshall Islands. In most developed countries, government spending as a percentage of GDP runs about 35%–50%.

Limits on Government Spending

Government spending is limited by the amount of tax revenue and the ability to borrow. For a country like the United States, this is not much of a limiting factor, as taxes are mandatory and US government debt is a popular vehicle for financial investment. Regardless of the political party in power, government spending tends to have an upward trajectory.

Government spending is often used to stimulate consumption during recessions because government often has the ability and will to spend when other sectors of the economy do not. The effectiveness of this spending—which often results in a deficit because the government is spending more than it generates in tax revenue—is hotly debated among the different schools of economic thought. Those economists influenced by the work of John Maynard Keynes tend to support government spending as a stimulus to the economy. The idea is that government spending has a multiplier effect: a dollar spent by the government helps increase the GDP by more than a dollar. Economists with a classical or libertarian bias often argue that government spending offsets more efficient private spending (e.g., the government should let you buy your TV in peace instead of taking your money off your hands through taxes) and should not be used as a tool of stimulus.

NET EXPORTS

Net exports, or exports minus imports, are the last spending variable in measuring GDP. Export of new domestic production adds to GDP. Imports, on the other hand, subtract from GDP. The United States typically runs a balance of trade deficit, so in most years net exports are deducted from, instead of added to, GDP. In recent years, export growth has helped to sustain GDP. Compared to most other nations, US net exports represent a very small percentage of economic activity. The United States engages in the second highest international trade by volume (after China), and relies heavily on trade for prosperity.

Exports and Economic Growth

Net exports may not be a real big deal in America, but for developing countries, net exports are the road to economic growth. China is a key example of a country dependent on net exports for continued growth. However, Chinese consumerism has been steadily making up a greater share of GDP for both goods and services.

Net exports are influenced by exchange rates and, like consumption and investment, also by interest rates. Appreciation of the dollar makes American goods relatively expensive, so exports decline and imports rise. Depreciation of the dollar, on the other hand, makes American goods relatively cheap, so exports increase and imports decrease. Interest rates impact net exports through their effect on the exchange rate. High interest rates in America lead to an appreciation of the dollar, which reduces net exports, but low American interest rates help to depreciate the dollar and encourage net exports.

APPROACHES TO GDP

Lies, Damned Lies, and Statistics

So far, we have looked at GDP as a sum of expenditures: add together consumer spending, private investment, government spending, and net exports, and voilà! The GDP. But this is not the only way to measure the growth of the economy. Economists can also use the income approach (adding together income) or the production approach (adding together outputs). Note that each of these approaches is meant to give the same answer—the GDP. They are not supposed to calculate different things. If you measure the economy using each of the three approaches, you should come up with roughly the same answer.

In addition, for economists to compare GDP from year to year, they also need to address the difference between the real and nominal GDP.

INCOME APPROACH TO GDP

If we can look at expenditures as a signal of economic growth (or contraction), we can also look at income. Theoretically, the GDP should remain the same whether you use the income approach or the expenditure approach (because income equals expenditures; saving is a form of expenditure in this calculation). The ability to engage in consumption, investment, government spending, and net exports derives from the income earned, producing domestic output. Again, income includes all of the rent, wages, interest, and profits earned by selling the factors of production in the factor market.

Measuring income is more complex than measuring spending, and this requires some mental gymnastics on the part of economists.

One reason is that profits flow to corporations, shareholders, and proprietors. Also, taxes and subsidies distort the difference between the price paid in the market and the income earned by producers. In the end, measuring income is a bit more complex for economists than measuring expenditures, but for now it is sufficient to conclude that income equals the sum of rent, wages, interest, and profits.

One last practical problem arises when measuring income versus spending. Producers and households have an incentive to underreport income in order to reduce their tax liability.

PRODUCTION OR OUTPUT APPROACH

Another way of calculating the GDP is to add together all of the production activity in a country. In this approach, the value added at each stage of the production process is calculated. For example, a car is the final output but the engineer's intermediate input has a value that can be determined. An obvious drawback to this approach is determining the difference between intermediate and final goods. Is a pound of sugar an intermediate or final good? The answer is, it depends on who is buying it and why.

In this approach, market and nonmarket production must both be valued. Market production is goods produced for sale in the marketplace (such as widgets produced by corporations). Nonmarket production includes services not for market sale (such as that provided by the government or nonprofits—for example, the free lunch program offered each summer by your local school). Nonmarket production can be difficult to value as it doesn't have a price tag attached to it, so generally it is considered to be the cost of production. US government agencies do not use this approach to calculate GDP.

NOMINAL VERSUS REAL GDP

The concepts of nominal and real appear throughout economics, and GDP is no exception. Nominal GDP is reported using current prices. In order for economists to make valid comparisons in GDP from year to year, the price changes that occur with time's passage have to be addressed. Real GDP reports output, holding prices constant. If the change in prices (inflation) is not accounted for in calculating GDP, results may be misleading—the economy may appear to be growing when in fact all that's happening is inflation.

Nominal GDP must be deflated in order to calculate real GDP. Assume a simple economy that produces multicolored beach balls. In 2022, the economy produced 100 beach balls that were all purchased by consumers at $1 apiece. In 2023, the economy produced 100 identical beach balls that were all purchased by consumers for $1.25 apiece. Given this information, nominal GDP for each year can be calculated by multiplying the number of beach balls by that year's current price, so in 2022 nominal GDP was $100, and in 2023 it was $125. An outside observer might come to the incorrect conclusion that output increased by 25%. The reality was that output did not change, but prices rose by 25%. To compare what really happened, prices must be held constant. Using 2022 prices, the real GDP for 2022 and 2023 is $100; in other words, real output remained constant.

The GDP Deflator

You can determine the overall inflation (or deflation) in an economy by dividing a specific year's nominal GDP by its real GDP. For example, if the nominal GDP was $125 and the real GDP was $100, then inflation was 25%.

REAL GDP CHANGES AND THE BUSINESS CYCLE

Buckle Your Seat Belts

Over the last fifty years, America has undergone alternating periods of recession and economic expansion. The ups and downs have occurred against a background of long-run economic growth. In other words, from year to year the GDP may go up and down overall but the trend is upward. Since 1960, the US real GDP has increased by more than $20 trillion.

EXPANSION AND CONTRACTION

Economists refer to this series of expansions and contractions as the business cycle (some economists prefer the term "fluctuation" since "cycle" implies a predictable pattern, which does not exist).

As the workforce and productivity grow, so does the economy's capacity to produce. This explains why the economy has grown over time. The periods of expansion and contraction are attributed to differences between total spending on output relative to the economy's long-term capacity to produce. During periods of expansion, spending increases to the point where the economy exceeds its long-run production capacity. Contractions occur as total spending decreases and excess productive capacity remains.

If you have ever been on a long car trip, you can understand the business cycle. Imagine cruising along a two-lane highway, going with the flow of traffic. This going with the flow is the norm and represents the average rate of economic growth. Occasionally, somebody will be moving a little too slowly, so you scan for oncoming traffic. If it's clear, you accelerate and pass the slower driver. Passing represents those periods where spending exceeds the productive capacity. Every once in a while, you make a mistake while trying to pass slower traffic. You scan for oncoming traffic and make your move, only to discover that a fully loaded eighteen-wheeler is barreling down the highway in the oncoming lane. You immediately switch back into your lane, shaking violently, and slow to thirty miles per hour, thankful that you are still alive. Events like this are representative of economic contractions. Eventually, you compose yourself and start to travel with the flow of traffic again.

Now, to really understand the business cycle, imagine that you are blindfolded the whole time and are relying on a myopic passenger who provides you with information about what is happening in an unknown language. To be sure, it would be an interesting ride. Why the blindfold and an unknown language? The language of economists and financial experts is often difficult to interpret.

The Four Stages of the Business Cycle

Economists generally point to four stages in the business cycle. The first is expansion, which occurs when the GDP grows month-over-month, and unemployment declines. Second is peak, which occurs when real GDP spending is at its highest—the period just before unemployment begins to rise and other economic indicators fall. Third is contraction, which occurs when GDP growth slows or declines. A recession is specifically defined as two consecutive quarters of declining real GDP. And fourth is trough, which is the period between contraction and expansion as GDP begins to recover. As this description makes clear, economists can only determine what stage the economy is in after it has happened.

THEORIES OF BUSINESS CYCLES

Economists disagree on exactly why the economy fluctuates as it does. Is the culprit external causes, such as wars? Or internal factors, such as business innovation? They also disagree on what should be done during downturns. How much should the government meddle? That depends on which economist you talk to.

- Milton Friedman's monetarists explain the business cycle as being caused by poor management of the money supply. Periods of overexpansion are produced by too much money, and periods of contraction are caused by too little money in circulation.
- Keynes explained the business cycle as being caused by "animal spirits" in businesses. Keynes's animal spirits represent the emotion that clouds rational decision-making. These animal spirits are expressed through businesses' willingness to invest. When businesses have high spirits, they invest heavily, only to fall into stages of low spirits where they are unwilling to invest.
- Most other theories explain the business cycle as ultimately being caused by spending changes, but one referred to as the Real Business Cycle Theory focuses on changes in productivity as being the ultimate cause of the cycle.

WHAT GDP DOESN'T TELL US

Money Isn't Everything

In a 1968 speech, the late presidential candidate Robert F. Kennedy stated the following about the weaknesses of our key measure of economic performance at that time, gross national product. The same weaknesses apply to GDP:

"Too much and for too long, we seemed to have surrendered personal excellence and community values in the mere accumulation of material things. Our gross national product...if we judge the United States of America by that...counts air pollution and cigarette advertising, and ambulances to clear our highways of carnage...It counts...armored cars for the police to fight the riots in our cities...

"Yet the gross national product does not allow for the health of our children, the quality of their education, or the joy of their play. It does not include the beauty of our poetry or the strength of our marriages, the intelligence of our public debate or the integrity of our public officials...It measures everything, in short, except that which makes life worthwhile. And it can tell us everything about America except why we are proud that we are Americans."

REAL GDP AND SOCIAL GOOD

Kennedy's point should be clear. GDP, for all of its inclusiveness, excludes many important things—not least of which is the value of unpaid labor such as caring for your children or elderly parents. However, consider the fact that as real GDP has increased, the burdens of scarcity and the incidence of absolute poverty have been lifted for millions of people. Yesterday's relative wealth is today's relative poverty. Compared to the lives of Americans of previous generations, the availability of healthcare, education, nutrition, sanitation, and housing has increased with the increases in real GDP. These have led to an increase in longevity.

The increase in real GDP has been accompanied by more leisure time as well. The average workweek has steadily declined, and the average number of vacation days has increased. As a measure of well-being, the GDP has both strengths and weaknesses.

GDP per Capita

GDP per capita is the GDP divided by the population. As an indicator of overall well-being, it is subject to a major flaw. GDP per capita gives no indication as to how income is distributed among the population. The United States and Norway both have high GDPs per capita, but the key difference is that US incomes are unequally distributed compared to Norway. High GDP per capita does not necessarily mean that there are not those in society living in relative poverty.

GDP AND THE ENVIRONMENT

Critics of GDP say that it does not take into account environmental degradation. Because GDP is focused on spending and output, it creates an incentive to pursue greater amounts of production in order for growth to continue. This growth can come at the cost of the environment. Deforestation, climate change, pollution, and other environmental ills are, according to critics of the measure, the logical outcome of this narrow-sighted focus on GDP. Others defend

GDP, stating that it is because of the increase in real GDP that people are wealthy enough and have the time to care for the environment. Today, the countries with the highest real GDPs are often the very ones that are doing the most to address the issues that environmentally conscious citizens raise.

Some countries are exploring measures called "green GDP" that take into account the environmental cost of economic growth.

OTHER MEASURES OF ECONOMIES

In response to complaints about what GDP measures, other formulas have been explored that address its shortcomings. Some of these include:

- Index of Sustainable Economic Welfare, which also calculates income distribution and pollution
- Genuine Progress Indicator, which seeks to measure the welfare of a country's citizens by including unpaid labor (household work, childcare, volunteer work) and other statistics
- Index of Social Health, which takes into account social well-being, such as drug use, homicide, and income inequality
- United Nations Human Development Index, which includes life expectancy and access to education
- Happy Planet Index, which tries to measure personal happiness or well-being instead of economic health

Money Talks

income inequality
The uneven distribution of income among households in a country.

KEY ECONOMIC INDICATORS

Crystal Ball by the Numbers

Economic indicators are top-level measurements that help economists, politicians, and analysts understand what's currently happening in the economy and what's likely to happen next. These key pieces of data most frequently come from the government, but they may also come from universities or nonprofits.

Most economic indicators don't work as stand-alone statistics. They give more information when looked at in combination with other numbers or over time. For example, knowing the unemployment rate right now isn't as valuable as knowing the trend in unemployment rates over the past three years. Other indicators are more useful when compared to specific benchmarks. For example, the Federal Reserve has set an inflation target rate of 2% annually, and compares this to the actual inflation rate to determine which actions to take.

LEADING, LAGGING, AND COINCIDENT INDICATORS

There are three kinds of economic indicators: leading, lagging, and coincident. Each type offers a different way to assess the direction of the economy, and what might be coming next.

Economic factors that change before the overall economy changes, offering some insight into what comes next, are called leading indicators. These indicators don't always pan out as expected, but decades of experience show us that they offer reliable predictive information. Commonly quoted leading indicators include:

- Durable goods orders, which looks at orders for big-ticket items like major appliances, cars, and industrial equipment
- Consumer confidence index, or CCI, measures consumer sentiments about the economy and their expectations for the economy in the near future
- Housing starts, which looks at new residential construction

When demand for new homes or durable goods increases, that indicates a strong economy ahead. When these indicators decline, they can signal an economic downturn.

Lagging indicators follow on the heels of a change in the economy. Analysts primarily use these indicators to confirm that a change is taking place. One commonly cited lagging indicator is the unemployment report as a measure of the strength of the economy. Here, unemployment refers to people who are not currently working but could be, calculated as the total number of unemployed people divided by the full labor force. When this number increases, it confirms existing economic struggle, and it typically doesn't decrease until the economy is well into its recovery.

Coincident indicators happen at the same time as changes occur in the economy. Like lagging indicators, coincident indicators help confirm the country's economic health. For example, when the economy is strong, people's incomes tend to increase. GDP is the most widely used coincident economic indicator. It tracks the overall wellness of the country's economy, measuring all the goods and services sold within that country during a particular period, usually a quarter or a year. Economists and market analysts track the GDP over time to measure the economy's health and direction.

Stock Traders Rely On Economic Indicators

Financial advisors and stock traders factor economic indicators into their investment decisions. The stock market reacts to indicator announcements, so having a good handle on what they mean gives savvy traders a clear edge.

SEVEN WEIRD ECONOMIC INDICATORS

Not all economic indicators are carefully calculated and compiled in stuffy rooms lined with supercomputers. Some of the most popular—and unexpected—indicators look directly at how people and events affect the economy and vice versa.

Hemlines

What do hemlines say about the economy? When hemlines go up and skirts get shorter, the economy and the stock market tend to be on the rise as well. Longer skirts coincide with declining stock prices and a sluggish economy. Some economists believe this lagging indicator holds true because people tend to show off more skin when times are good.

The Library

The Library Indicator gauges the strength of the economy based on the number of library visitors. This phenomenon, discovered by librarians rather than economists, shows that library use increases during recession. People visit more, check out more books, and use more online library services during tough economic times.

Men's Underwear
According to former Federal Reserve chair Alan Greenspan, men's underwear sales can predict the direction of the economy. Since it's the piece of clothing people don't see, it's the last purchase people would need to make, the theory goes. People cut back on non-necessities when they're facing financial pressures, which happens in a weak economy. As men's underwear sales start to decline, it signals economic trouble.

Philadelphia Wins
Do baseball outcomes affect the economy? Turns out that whenever Philadelphia wins a title, the economy tanks. Consider the history of their rare wins, starting with the Philadelphia Athletics winning a championship in 1929, after which the country plunged into the Great Depression. Fast forward to 1980 when the Phillies won the World Series and recession hit the nation. Or 2008, when they clinched their second World Series and an economic crisis followed. What's the connection? Most economists believe it's a weird coincidence, but breathed a sigh of relief that the Phillies didn't win in 2022.

Lipstick
The Lipstick Theory predicts recession; it has been doing so since 2001. During tough economic times people cut back on spending, but look for small affordable luxuries like lipstick. Lipstick sales tend to increase as the economy begins to tighten up. The one exception:

the post–COVID-19 lipstick boom, which had more to do with freedom from masking than pending recession.

Big Macs

The Economist developed the Big Mac Index back in 1986 as an economic measure that compared relative purchase power among different currencies. Each country's currency is compared to its cost of a Big Mac to determine whether that currency might be overvalued or undervalued. Since Big Macs hold a relatively steady store of value, it acts like a benchmark across currency.

Cardboard Boxes

The Cardboard Box Index acts as a leading indicator to predict the state of the economy. Product manufacturers rely on cardboard boxes to deliver their goods. When they need more cardboard boxes, it's a sign that people are ordering and purchasing more, indicating an economic uptick. Conversely, when cardboard box production drops off, it can signal impending economic downturn.

THE US DEFICIT AND NATIONAL DEBT

Keeping the Wheels Turning

Deficit and debt both feel negative, but both can be positive for normal government functioning. While many people use the terms interchangeably, they don't mean the same thing. The deficit is the difference between money received and money spent, sort of like a business loss or a personal budget overage. The debt is the money owed, just like business and personal loans. Running at a deficit and having debt keep the country running, and neither signals a weak economy. And it's been that way since almost the beginning.

THE US DEFICIT

The budget deficit occurs when government expenditures exceed revenues—basically when the government spends more money than it has. It's sort of like your household budget: when the money you spend ends up being more than your income, you're running at a budget deficit. Sometimes that happens because of timing, like you need groceries before your paycheck hits your bank account so you have to turn to a credit card. Sometimes it's because unexpected expenses popped up, like a fender bender or vet bills.

For fiscal year 2023, the federal deficit hit $1.7 trillion; government spending hit $6.13 trillion while revenue collection only reached $4.44 trillion. If things had gone the other way, and revenues exceeded expenses, there would be a budget surplus.

What Causes a Deficit?

The US government has been running at a deficit since 2002 following its last surplus for fiscal year 2001. Whether the government faces a surplus or a deficit depends on many factors, including overall health of the economy, government spending initiatives, costs of servicing the national debt, current tax laws, IRS collection (including those from audits), and employment levels.

Certain scenarios are more likely to cause budget deficits, such as lowered taxes for high earners and corporations, increased military spending, higher government subsidies for businesses and industries, and unexpected events such as the COVID-19 pandemic.

How to Improve the Deficit

Just like with your household budget, there are two ways to improve a government budget deficit: increase revenues, which can mean raising taxes, or reduce expenses, which can mean cutting government spending on programs. Either of those can have huge impacts on the overall economy, and it can be hard for Congress to agree on which path to take.

When the economy is flourishing, deficits generally decrease due to increased tax revenues and reduced need for spending on government programs such as federal unemployment insurance. Weaker economies typically increase the deficit, and programs needed to improve the economy and spur economic growth can temporarily spike the deficit until they produce the desired results.

NATIONAL DEBT

As of October 2023, the United States has $33.2 trillion in debt, 123% of the country's GDP. More than 20% of that, around $7 trillion, is owned by other arms of the US government, with the Federal Reserve holding the largest chunk.

Servicing this debt, meaning making the interest and principal payments as they come due, is one of the country's biggest expenses. Interest payments alone come to more than $395 billion a year. But being in debt is nothing new for the United States.

Since its very first days, the US government has been in debt, with war often stoking huge increases. The new country borrowed more than $75 million to finance the Revolutionary War. The national debt bounced up and down over the years but skyrocketed from $65 million in 1860 to $1 billion in 1863 to $2.7 billion by 1865 due to the costs of the Civil War. World War I expenses ballooned the national debt to $27 billion. And World War II caused another seismic jump to $260 billion in debt. But war isn't the only driver of the national debt. The COVID-19 pandemic drove the debt to new heights, as government spending increased dramatically to keep the country and the American people afloat.

The debt to GDP ratio is a key measure of national debt. A ratio of 100% means that the GDP can cover the entire debt, a ratio lower than that means the GDP covers more than the national debt, and a ratio higher than 100% means that debt exceeds the GDP.

Types of US Government Debt

The US government builds up debt by issuing bonds, which are basically loan obligations that come with interest payments and due dates (called maturity dates). Unlike mortgages and other types of personal loans, government bonds make periodic interest payments for the whole life of the debt but only pay the principal back at the very end in one lump sum.

The US issues three basic types of bonds: Treasury bills, which mature in one year or less; Treasury notes, which mature in two to ten years; and Treasury bonds, which mature in twenty to thirty years. The interest payments on these bonds add to the budget deficit, as that money has to be paid out every year.

Who Holds the US Debt?

As of September 2023, the countries owning the most US Treasury securities according to the Treasury.gov website include Japan ($1.1 trillion), China ($778 billion), United Kingdom ($669 billion), Luxembourg ($374 billion), Belgium ($317 billion), Cayman Islands ($315 billion), and Ireland ($295 billion). The largest holder of Treasury debt by far is the US Federal Reserve with around $5 trillion.

Full Faith and Credit

The United States offers an unconditional guarantee to honor all interest and principal payments when they issue bonds. These unsecured loans (meaning there's no collateral behind them) rely on the full faith and credit, the country's reputation for always making payments as they come due.

International Debt

When it comes to countries in debt, the US is not the only one, though we do have the most by far. Virtually all countries have debt, and the combined international debt is more than $300 trillion as of 2023. The countries with the highest national debt (in US dollars) include:

1. United States, $33.2 trillion
2. China, $14.2 trillion
3. Japan, $10.1 trillion
4. France, $3.5 trillion
5. United Kingdom, $3.1 trillion
6. Italy, $2.9 trillion
7. Germany, $2.8 trillion
8. Canada, $2.5 trillion
9. India, $2.0 trillion
10. Spain, $1.7 trillion

Though it's not the highest in terms of dollars, Japan has by far the highest debt to GDP ratio of 256%.

UNEMPLOYMENT DEFINED

Where Did My Job Go?

One of the most gratifying things that you can hear is, "We like you, and you're the right fit for this company. Congratulations, you're hired!" One of the worst things you can hear is, "You're fired." Unemployment can make economics suddenly even more relevant to your life. Economists define, measure, classify, evaluate, and seek to understand this all-too-common phenomenon. Many economists have made it their life's work to minimize the problem of unemployment, and policymakers are under political pressure to do so as well.

WHAT UNEMPLOYMENT IS AND IS NOT

According to the Census Bureau, the 2022 US population was approximately 333 million, of which approximately 169.8 million were employed. How many were unemployed? It might come as a surprise to you that the answer to that question cannot be determined from the information given. True, you can infer that 163.2 million did not work, but that does not necessarily mean that they were all unemployed. To determine the number of unemployed people, you must first define the term "unemployment."

Persons sixteen years of age or older are considered unemployed if they have actively searched for work in the last four weeks, but are not currently employed. The employed are those who have worked at least one hour in the previous two weeks. People who meet neither criterion are not considered in the labor force, which includes only the number of employed persons plus the number of unemployed persons. The unemployment rate that you hear quoted in the news is not a percentage of the population, but a percentage of the labor force that is not currently employed.

MEASURING UNEMPLOYMENT

The US Department of Labor's Bureau of Labor Statistics (BLS) monitors unemployment in the United States. Once a month, the Census Bureau conducts the Current Population Survey. Approximately 60,000 sample households are briefly questioned about their participation in the labor force. The BLS uses the data from the survey to calculate the various employment statistics used by economists and policymakers.

Unemployment Data

The latest unemployment and labor force data can be found at www.bls.gov. The Bureau of Labor Statistics website allows you to access hundreds of tables, graphs, press releases, and research articles.

Economists also look at payroll employment records, new claims for unemployment insurance, and other data to get a complete picture of the country's unemployment. Policymakers also look at the weekly hours worked in manufacturing. Declines in the weekly hours worked indicates that factories are idling and may be laying off workers. Increases in weekly hours worked may indicate that firms will hire in the future.

The BLS uses the survey data to calculate the labor force participation rate and the employment-to-population ratio. The labor force participation rate is the percentage of the working age population classified as either employed or unemployed. In the United States, the average labor force participation rate is about 63%. The employment-to-population ratio is the percentage of the working age population that is classified as employed.

UNEMPLOYMENT CLASSIFIED

Because of unemployment's narrow definition, many people that you might consider unemployed or underemployed are not captured in the official unemployment statistic:

- People ready and available to work who have conducted a job search within the past twelve months, but have not searched in the last four weeks
- People who have given up the job search in frustration
- Full-time workers who have lost jobs but have been rehired as part-time workers

Types of Unemployment

Economists make qualitative distinctions in the reasons for various classifications of unemployment. Not all unemployment is the same. Some types are actually positive for the individual and the economy. Other types are bad for the individual but benefit society. Last, there is one type of unemployment that is both bad for the individual and costly to society. The three types of unemployment are frictional, structural, and cyclical.

Frictional unemployment occurs when people voluntarily enter the labor force, or when they are between jobs for which they are qualified. It is frictional because the labor market does not automatically match up all available jobs with all available workers. Instead, a job search requires time for the right worker to find the right job. Both workers and society benefit when job applicants are matched to the appropriate job. The rate of frictional unemployment is relatively low, and as technology increases and search times diminish, it becomes even lower. The advent of online job search sites and social networking has reduced job search times for many workers.

Structural unemployment occurs when job seekers' skill sets are not in demand because of geography or obsolescence. As industries die out in certain regions of the country or relocate to other regions, the workers may not be able to move with the job. This leaves workers with a skill set that is no longer in demand. These workers must either retrain or accept a lower-paying job in an industry that requires less skill. Structural unemployment is often the outcome of what economist Joseph Schumpeter called creative destruction. As innovation occurs, old technologies and industries are destroyed, which frees up the resources for the new technology and its industry. The solution for structural unemployment is education and retraining.

Cyclical unemployment, the most insidious form, occurs because of contractions in the business cycle. During periods of recession, the official unemployment rate increases as cyclical unemployment adds to the always-present frictional and structural rates of unemployment.

The real problem with cyclical unemployment is that it creates a feedback loop. As one group becomes cyclically unemployed, they cut back on spending, which leads to more cyclical unemployment. Policymakers respond to cyclical unemployment with discretionary fiscal and monetary policy. In addition, automatic stabilizers like unemployment compensation help to dampen the feedback loop by allowing affected workers to have some capacity for spending. Ultimately the goal of policymakers is to eliminate cyclical unemployment altogether.

Full Employment

When the economy is producing at its optimum capacity, it's operating at full employment. Economists associate full employment with the natural rate of unemployment. The natural rate hypothesis advanced by Nobel economists Milton Friedman and Edmund Phelps suggests that in the long run, there is a level of unemployment that the economy maintains independent of the inflation rate. The idea is that, left alone, the economy will maintain full employment and experience the natural rate of unemployment most of the time.

WHY UNEMPLOYMENT IS BAD

Unemployment creates a measurable cost for the economy and individuals. The opportunity cost of unemployment is immense when considering the scale of the US economy.

When workers are unemployed, they are unable to produce output. According to Okun's Law, a theory posited by the economist Arthur Okun, for every 1% that the official unemployment rate exceeds the natural rate of unemployment, there is a 2% drop in GDP. While this theory doesn't always work accurately, economists use it as a rule of thumb to predict the effects of unemployment on the economy.

Personal and Social Costs of Unemployment

The costs to the individual are heavy as well. An extended period of unemployment can wipe out a family's personal savings and leave them in debt. Unemployment disrupts the normal flow of life and, if prolonged, can possibly lead to health and psychological problems for affected individuals. Also, the incidence of family violence is directly related to changes in the unemployment rate. Furthermore, periods of high unemployment are also associated with increases in the divorce rate and child abandonment.

Prolonged, pervasive unemployment is directly linked to crime and civil unrest. Areas plagued with persistent high unemployment are also plagued with both violent crime and property crime. A trip to America's inner cities provides the anecdotal evidence for this. Much of the unrest in the developing world coincides with high rates of unemployment. It is a very rare day when someone takes the morning off from work to riot or blow something up. Unemployment, it seems, creates the necessary condition for many of the world's problems.

INFLATION DEFINED

The Incredible Shrinking Dollar

Were you frustrated when gas prices suddenly rose? The increase in gas prices probably created some hardship as you altered your spending in order to accommodate its higher cost. It's not just gas prices climbing, but the price of almost everything you buy suddenly and unexpectedly increases. If you are on a fixed income, then there is only so much altering you can do to a budget before you realize that high prices are killing your finances. Inflation is a phenomenon that you need to understand if you want to comprehend how the economy works.

WHAT IS INFLATION?

No word strikes more fear into the hearts of central bankers than inflation. Defined as a general increase in prices or as a decrease in money's purchasing power, inflation affects everyone in the economy. Governments, businesses, and households are subject to inflation's influence. Inflation is created by excessive demand or by increases in producers' per-unit costs, but it is sustained by too much money in circulation. Left unchecked, inflation can have cataclysmic results for a society.

Measuring Inflation

Inflation is the rate of increase in the average price level of the economy. To measure inflation first requires that the price level be measured. Economists have come up with different ways to measure the general price level in the economy, and therefore, inflation. The most often cited measure of inflation is the change in the consumer price index (CPI). In addition, economists and policymakers pay attention to changes in the producer price index (PPI) and personal consumption expenditure (PCE) deflator.

The CPI is a market basket approach to measuring the price level and inflation published by the BLS. The CPI measures the average cost of food, clothing, shelter, energy, transportation, and healthcare that the average urban consumer buys. Imagine that you are given a shopping list of thousands of different items. You are then told to research and write down the price of each specific item, and afterward add them all together. The total cost of the list would represent an average price level. Further assume that a year later you took the same list and repeated the process. Increases in the shopping list's total would represent inflation.

The PPI is similar to the CPI, but instead of consumer prices, the PPI looks at producer prices. The PPI includes all domestic production of goods and services. Unlike the CPI, the PPI also includes the prices of goods sold by one producer to another. Changes in the PPI can be used as a predictor of future changes in the CPI. Before consumer prices change, the producer price changes. Because it predicts changes in the CPI, the government and central bank use the PPI to create fiscal and monetary policy in anticipation of possible consumer inflation.

The PCE deflator is a broad measure of consumer inflation published by the BEA. Unlike the CPI, which measures a fixed market basket, the PCE deflator measures all of the goods and services consumed by households and nonprofit institutions, a more comprehensive measure. This better reflects consumers' tendency to substitute more expensive items with less expensive items and their tendency to vary consumption as time passes.

TYPES OF INFLATION

There are two primary types of inflation: demand-pull and cost-push. Understanding which type of inflation is occurring at any given point in time is important if policymakers want to respond appropriately. The two types of inflation are not mutually exclusive, so it is possible for both to occur simultaneously. Left untreated, inflation can cause a wage-price spiral or even hyperinflation.

Demand-Pull Inflation

Demand-pull inflation occurs when spending on goods and services drives up prices. In other words, aggregate demand is greater than aggregate supply. Demand-pull inflation is fueled by income, so efforts to stop it involve reducing consumers' income or giving consumers more incentive to save than to spend.

Demand-pull inflation persists if the public or foreign sector reinforces it. Low taxes and profligate government spending exacerbate demand-pull inflation. A failure of the central bank to reign in the money supply also makes the demand-pull inflation worse.

Demand-pull inflation can spread across borders as well. China's and India's economic growth not only puts pressure on prices within their own economies, but also prices worldwide as the demand for imports increase.

If government spending is financed by printing currency or by the central bank monetizing the debt, demand-pull inflation can become hyperinflation. Hyperinflation is defined as a quick, extreme monthly inflation spike of 50% or greater. Hyperinflation may be accompanied by the government or central bank issuing too much money, leading to a rapid increase in the money supply, further stoking the issue.

Monetizing the Debt

Monetizing the debt refers to the process by which the central bank buys new government debt, thus increasing the supply of money in circulation. When debt is monetized, the government is able to spend without raising taxes or borrowing from the private sector. The downside is that debt monetization can be extremely inflationary.

Cost-Push Inflation

Cost-push inflation occurs when the price of inputs increases. Businesses must acquire raw materials, labor, energy, and capital to operate. If the price of these were to rise, it would reduce the ability of producers to generate output because their unit cost of production had increased. If these increases in production cost are relatively large and pervasive, the effect is to simultaneously create higher inflation, reduce real GDP, and increase the unemployment rate.

If cost-push inflation has a bright side, it is the fact that it is self-limiting. Cost-push inflation is associated with decreases in GDP. The decreased GDP and resulting high unemployment help to bring producer prices back down. The trick to combating cost-push inflation is realizing that it is not demand-pull. The policy prescription for each is different, and applying the wrong prescription can create more problems than it solves.

It is the unemployment issue that usually spurs policymakers to action. If they respond to the increased unemployment by increasing spending, the inflation problem is made worse. A wage-price spiral can result if the policy responses create more demand for goods and services at the same time that unit costs are rising. It's best policy to let cost-push inflation run its natural course.

Good Inflation

A small amount of inflation is considered healthy for the economy, as the anticipation that prices will rise increases demand. This increased demand helps the economy expand. But when inflation jumps higher, demand increases too much (as people anticipate much higher prices), creating demand-pull inflation and ever-higher prices. The magic number seems to be 2%. At a 2% annual rate of inflation, prices are relatively stable and slow growing. A 2% inflation rate results in prices doubling about every thirty-six years.

INFLATION: WINNERS AND LOSERS

Or When You Should Borrow Instead of Save

Inflation creates winners and losers. Knowing who wins is important for understanding why it is sometimes allowed to persist. When inflation is expected and stable, it is rather benign. People and institutions can plan for it and build it into their decision-making. If inflation is unexpected, it creates a win-lose situation in society. Who stands to gain from inflation?

BENEFITING FROM INFLATION

First consider what inflation is: a general increase in prices and a corresponding decrease in money's purchasing power. Borrowers benefit from a general increase in prices or a reduction in purchasing power. When individuals, businesses, and governments borrow, it is usually at a fixed rate of interest that had some expected level of inflation built into it. If higher-than-expected inflation occurs, then the real value of the borrower's debt is reduced.

Assume that banks lend billions of dollars at a fixed nominal interest rate of 6%. If inflation were to unexpectedly increase from 3% to 6%, then borrowers' real interest rate paid would be reduced from 3% to 0%. In simpler terms, the money that was lent was more precious than the money being repaid.

Another group that benefits from an increase in consumer prices in the short run is producers. When unexpected inflation occurs, consumer prices rise while wages paid to employees remain relatively stable. This allows producers to experience higher profits for a time until wages adjust to reflect the higher prices consumers are paying.

Overprinting and Inflation

In the past, many governments in the developing world tried erasing their foreign debts by overprinting their currency. Faced with much external debt, governments would devalue their currency in order to satisfy the debt. Given the current size of the US debt, some fear that the American government might be tempted to do something similar. Most developed nations have independent central banks to act as a check on government's incentive to overprint currency. In the United States, the Federal Reserve is somewhat insulated from political pressure and can constrain the money supply when government's incentives are to expand it.

LOSING WITH INFLATION

Inflation harms more than helps. Lenders and savers both lose when inflation exceeds expectations. Both earn interest rates that assume some rate of inflation, and when the actual rate exceeds the expected rate, savers and lenders are harmed. Maybe you save money in a bank CD. Assume you purchase a $1,000 one-year simple CD that pays 4% nominal interest. If inflation increases unexpectedly from 2% to 5%, then the real interest rate you earn is approximately -1%. You're worse off than when you started. In nominal terms you still made $40 of interest. The problem is that the $1,040 that you now have has less purchasing power than the $1,000 you started with.

Inflation is thought to be harder on those with lower incomes. People with low incomes tend to have more of their wealth in the form of cash than do those with higher incomes. High-income earners have cash to be sure, but they also are more likely to have much of their wealth in other real and financial assets. For lower-income households, inflation exacts a heavier toll because it destroys the value of their chief asset, which is cash. The higher-income earners are able to offset some of inflation's effect by holding assets that actually appreciate with inflation.

Those living on fixed incomes are also harmed by inflation. During periods of unanticipated inflation, fixed-income earners see their real incomes decline. Professionals on a fixed salary or retirees living on a fixed pension lose purchasing power as long as the rate of inflation exceeds the rate at which their pay increases. To mitigate some of these effects, employers, or in the case of Social Security recipients, the government, may adjust pay to inflation through the use of cost-of-living adjustments (COLA). Even with COLA, fixed-income earners are still harmed by inflation, as the cost adjustment lags behind inflation. During periods of higher-than-expected inflation, fixed-income earners are forever playing a game where their pay increases are too little and come too late. For several years, inflation outpaced American wages, but that trend finally began to turn around in September 2023 (though there's still a lot of catching up to do).

The Restaurant Menu As Inflation Indicator

When restaurants laminate their menus, they are not only protecting them from spills, but they are also testifying that prices are relatively stable. When inflation is out of control, restaurants must continually update their prices, so they do not want to fix prices on the menu. Unlike most restaurant prices, seafood prices are highly volatile; that is why they are usually priced on a chalkboard.

Inflation creates practical problems for individuals and businesses in an economy. Because money is quickly losing value, consumers must engage in transactions more frequently as they rush to spend whatever money they have. The increase in transactions creates what is called shoe-leather costs. You wear out your shoes quicker when inflation is present because of the increase in your transactions. Inflation also poses a problem for producers who constantly have to re-price their goods as inflation continues. Remember that there is no such thing as a free lunch. Placing prices on goods is not free. If inflation is high, then significant costs are created as businesses pay employees to re-price their items. Persistent inflation results in forgone output as labor resources are put to the task of keeping up with ever-changing prices.

DISINFLATION AND DEFLATION

Popping the Balloon

One of the triumphs of Fed policy came in the 1980s when the central bank under the direction of then-chair Paul Volcker raised interest rates and helped bring inflation down from double digits to a more modest 4%, thus ending the period known as the Great Inflation. If you were around at that time, then you will recall that the Fed action also resulted in the worst recession in decades. In retrospect, many economists agree that the reduction in inflation or disinflation that resulted was worth the cost of recession. From the 1980s onward, inflation remained relatively low and stable and ushered in an economic era known as the Great Moderation.

DISINFLATION

Disinflation is beneficial to an economy for several reasons. Disinflation reduces pressure to increase wages, as prices are more stable. Disinflation also results in lower, more stable interest rates, which makes capital investment less costly and easier to plan. Arguably the most important outcome of disinflation is that producers' and consumers' inflationary expectations are lowered, which results in a profoundly more stable economic environment.

The Role of Expectations

One of the interesting features of economics is the possibility for self-fulfilling prophecies. In the realm of inflation, fear or hubris is often realized with changes in the rate of inflation. The fear of inflation or the general expectation that inflation will occur is often enough to spark an inflationary period. Consumers fearful of inflation will spend more and save less, which results in demand-pull inflation. The resulting demand-pull inflation reinforces the expectation of future inflation, and wage earners demand higher nominal wages to offset the effects. This of course results in cost-push inflation. If policymakers fail to manage the expectations of inflation, a higher expected inflation rate embeds itself into the economic consciousness. With this higher expected rate of inflation, the economy is not able to produce as much output as it otherwise would and faces higher prices than it otherwise should.

Central bank authorities try to manage not only actual inflation, but more importantly, the expectation of future inflation. Because the fear of inflation is often enough to create it, policymakers are in the business of acting as a psychologist to the economy.

It is not enough to talk the talk when it comes to managing expectations, however; the Fed must walk the walk. If you have ever dealt with children, you know that words without action are meaningless. A parent may respond to a teenager's rude behavior by threatening, "If you don't stop misbehaving, you're grounded." If the rude behavior continues and the parent doesn't act on the threat, the parent's credibility is undermined. A parent who consistently follows through is much more credible.

Likewise, the Federal Reserve bolsters its credibility when it raises interest rates in response to inflation fears, but loses credibility when it fails to respond forcibly to the possibility of inflation. The Fed's credibility as an inflation fighter was greatly reinforced by Paul Volcker's leadership as chair because he said what he meant and meant what he said.

DEFLATION

If inflation is bad and disinflation is better, then deflation must be best, right? Wrong. Deflation occurs when the average price level is declining and money's purchasing power is increasing. What could be wrong with that? The problem with deflation is that it creates a perverse set of incentives in the economy. If prices are steadily declining, then consumers delay their purchase of durable goods as the deals just keep getting better as time passes. If this behavior continues, manufacturing grinds to a halt and widespread unemployment results. The unemployment would then reinforce the deflation, as fewer and fewer consumers would be willing and able to purchase goods and services. Producers respond similarly to deflation by delaying investment and compounding the effects of the delayed consumption.

Deflation poses a policy dilemma for central banks that primarily use interest rates to influence economic activity. In response to increased inflation, central banks raise interest rates to reduce the flow of credit and cool inflation pressure. There is no upper limit to how high an interest rate can go, but the opposite is not true. Given deflation, central banks will lower interest rates to encourage investment and consumption. If the lower interest rates do not have the desired effect, central banks will continue to lower them until they hit what economists refer to as the zero bound. Once interest rates are at zero, they cannot go lower.

John Maynard Keynes referred to this weakness in monetary policy as liquidity trap. If consumers and investors will not borrow or lend at 0% interest, then you are out of options.

The Deflation Solution

The solution for deflation is to create inflation. Milton Friedman suggested that in economies with an inconvertible fiat money standard, deflation should never be a problem. All the monetary authorities would need to do is print money, or in the case of economies with independent central banks, monetize the debt, and the deflation would end. It's been said that this policy is like a government ending deflation by dropping cash from helicopters over the landscape.

AGGREGATE DEMAND AND AGGREGATE SUPPLY

The Economist's Crystal Ball

Once you understand the concepts of supply and demand, GDP, unemployment, and inflation, you have a toolkit for understanding the economic fluctuations that occur. The aggregate demand and aggregate supply model will allow you to analyze the entire economy. You'll even be able to predict what might happen given certain events. If you're not careful, you might end up sounding like an economist the next time the Fed raises interest rates.

AGGREGATE DEMAND

Recall that demand is the willingness and ability of consumers to purchase a good or service at various prices in a specific period of time. Aggregate demand (AD) is a similar concept, but has some important distinctions. AD is the demand for all final domestic production in a country. Instead of just households, AD comes from all sectors of the economy. Furthermore, AD relates the price level to the amount of real GDP instead of price to quantity.

The relationship between the price level and the amount of real GDP is inverse. The higher the price level, the less real GDP is demanded, and the lower the price level, the more real GDP is demanded. This is true because as the price level rises, money and other financial assets lose purchasing power. Fewer people demand our exports, and corresponding higher interest rates discourage investment and consumption. As the price level decreases, purchasing power increases, exports become more affordable to foreigners, and the corresponding lower interest rates encourage investment and consumption.

Changes in AD occur when consumption, private investment, government spending, or net exports change independent of changes in the price level. For example, if the general mood of the country improves and consumers and businesses are feeling more confident, they will consume and invest more, regardless of the price level. This increase in consumption and investment increases AD.

Likewise, increases in government spending or net exports also tend to increase AD. Reductions in any of the spending components of GDP will tend to suppress AD. If government raises the average tax rates on income, households' disposable income is reduced and they consume less, which reduces AD.

AGGREGATE SUPPLY

Supply is the willingness and ability of producers to generate the output of some good or service at various prices in a specific time period. Aggregate supply is a much broader concept than supply because it is inclusive of all domestic production, not just a singular good or service. Like an individual firm, an economy has a production function that relates the amount of labor employed with the amount of output or real GDP that the economy can produce with some fixed level of capital. In the short run, the amount of real GDP supplied is directly related to the price level. However, in the long run, the amount of real GDP producers collectively supply is independent of the price level.

The Short Run

Why do firms respond in the short run to price level increases by producing more output and vice versa? Before answering this question, it's important to recall what is meant by short run in the macroeconomic sense. The short run is the period of time in which input prices (primarily nominal wages) do not adjust to price level changes. If the economy experiences unexpected inflation, the short run is the period in which wages remain fixed before finally adjusting to the inflation. During this period, firms realize higher profits as their output earns ever-higher prices while they maintain the same wage payments to their workers. Firms respond to the higher profits by increasing their collective output, or real GDP. In response to decreases in the price level, firms reduce output as they experience losses. This relationship is called the short-run aggregate supply (SRAS).

SRAS is affected by changes in per-unit production cost. As per-unit production costs fall, the economy is able to produce more real GDP at every price level, and as unit costs rise, the economy's ability to generate real GDP is reduced. In true economic style, per-unit production costs themselves are subject to influence by productivity, regulation, taxes, subsidies, and inflationary expectations.

- Productivity is output per worker and as it increases, per-unit costs fall. Decreases in productivity lead to higher per-unit production costs.
- Regulations place compliance costs on businesses and act to reduce SRAS. For example, to reduce sulfur dioxide emissions, factories must pay for smokestack scrubbers, which means that money cannot be used to increase output.
- Taxes on producers directly reduce their capacity to produce, while subsidies increase their productive capacity.

Inflationary Expectations and Changes in SRAS

Inflationary expectations influence the unit costs of production and therefore SRAS. As inflationary expectations increase, workers demand higher wages, lenders demand higher interest rates, and commodity prices increase as a result of speculation. The outcome is for SRAS to be reduced by inflationary expectations. Decreases in inflationary expectations have an opposite effect and serve to increase SRAS.

The Long Run

In the long run, the price level is irrelevant to the level of real GDP firms are willing to produce. The long run is the period of time in which input prices adjust to changes in the price level. Unlike the short run, where increases in the price level induce more output, in the long run firms do not realize higher profits and thus have no incentive to increase output. Why? Input prices match the increases in the price level. Therefore, in the long run, firms' input prices (wages) increase at the same rate as general price inflation, and in real terms are constant. The independence of real GDP from the price level is referred to as long-run aggregate supply (LRAS).

Changes in LRAS

LRAS is directly influenced by the availability of the factors of production. If land, labor, capital, and entrepreneurship increase, then LRAS increases. Decreases in the availability of these resources reduce LRAS. Increases in LRAS are characterized as economic growth. Decreases in LRAS represent a long-term economic decline. The medieval Black Death that wiped out a third of the European population is an example of an event that reduces LRAS. The invention of the steam engine exemplifies the type of technology that expands LRAS.

MACROECONOMIC EQUILIBRIUM

Putting It All Together

Macroeconomic equilibrium occurs when the real GDP that is demanded by the different economic sectors equals the real GDP that producers supply. Short-run equilibriums occur when AD equals SRAS, and long-run equilibriums occur when AD equals LRAS. Changes in macroeconomic equilibrium occur when there are changes in AD, SRAS, or LRAS.

Increases in AD relative to SRAS result in both increased price level and increased real GDP in the short run, but just increased price level in the long run.

THE INTERPLAY OF AD, LRAS, AND SRAS

As consumers, businesses, government, and the foreign sector demand more scarce output, firms respond to the increased price level by increasing output. In the long run, wages adjust to the increased price level, and GDP returns to its long-run potential at a higher price level. Demand-pull inflation results from increases in AD. Decreases in AD result in the opposite: As AD decreases relative to SRAS, both real GDP and price level fall. In the long run, wages and other input prices adjust to the lower price level and the economy returns to its long-run potential GDP at a lower price level than when the process began.

Unemployment and Aggregate Demand Changes

What happens to unemployment as aggregate demand (AD) changes? Increases in AD lead to increases in real GDP. The increase in real GDP creates more demand for labor and reduces the unemployment rate. The reduced unemployment comes at the cost of an increase in the price level.

Changes in SRAS relative to AD also lead to changes in real GDP and price level. Unlike AD changes, which lead to GDP and price level moving in the same direction, SRAS changes result in GDP and price level moving opposite from each other.

- An increase in SRAS relative to AD will lead to a higher real GDP at a lower price level because, as production costs fall, firms are more willing to produce more output at each and every price level.
- A decrease in SRAS relative to AD leads to the economic condition known as stagflation. Stagflation occurs when GDP decreases are combined with increases in the price level. When the costs of production rise, firms produce less output at each and every price level.

THE CLASSICAL VIEW

Prior to the Great Depression, traditional economic thought could be described as "classical." Today, classical refers not only to those economists with pre-Depression notions of the economy, but also can be used to describe a much broader group of economists who favor market-based solutions to economic problems. The classical camp espouses what is best described as a laissez-faire philosophy.

The classical view of the economy is one that emphasizes the inherent stability of AD and aggregate supply. Efficient markets are able to reach equilibrium conditions quickly and effectively, so periods of extended unemployment are not possible. When consumers stop spending, they are saving instead. This increased saving reduces the real interest rate and spurs investment in capital, so any decreases in consumption are offset by increases in investment. This leads to the conclusion that AD is stable.

If shocks do occur to the economy, flexible wages and prices allow the economy to quickly adjust to changes in the price level, as rational economic actors take into account all available information when making decisions. For example, workers will accept lower wages in response to deflation and demand higher wages in response to inflation. This quick response implies that the economy tends to remain at its long-run equilibrium of full employment. Government interference is not warranted given this assumption, and as a result, laissez-faire is the best policy.

Say's Law

One of the assumptions at the heart of classical economic thought is Say's law. French economist Jean-Baptiste Say believed that supply creates its own demand, and as a result, surpluses could not be sustained in a market economy.

The classical response to economic recession is to do nothing. A decrease in AD leads to lower GDP and a lower price level. The resulting high unemployment puts downward pressure on wages as workers will willingly go back to work for less money. These lower wages encourage firms to increase SRAS, and the economy returns to equilibrium at full employment. No government action is necessary as market forces are working to bring the economy back to full employment.

The classical response to inflation is also to do nothing. Increased AD leads to a higher GDP and higher price level. As the unemployment rate falls below the natural rate, considerable upward wage pressure results. With few unemployed workers available, firms compete with each other for already-employed workers; this means offering higher wages to entice them to leave their current jobs. This intense competition for workers and other resources increases the costs of production for businesses. They eventually reduce production, and the economy returns to full employment at a higher but stable price level. Once again, no government intervention is necessary because market forces return the economy to its long-run full-employment equilibrium.

THE KEYNESIAN VIEW AND FISCAL POLICY

The Meddler

Britain's John Maynard Keynes was a classically trained economist who eventually concluded that the classical assumptions did not describe the reality of his day. During the Depression, Keynes wrote *The General Theory of Employment, Interest, and Money.* In it he challenged the prevailing assumptions and concluded that government intervention was warranted in the case of the Depression. He observed that saving did not instantly translate into new capital investment. Savings gluts could and did occur, and this implied that AD was inherently unstable, as decreases in consumption were not offset by increases in investment.

Free-Market Enemy?

Keynes is a polarizing figure in economics. His ideas challenged the status quo, and he is seen by many as the enemy of free-market economics. The writings of Friedrich von Hayek and Ludwig von Mises of the Austrian school of economic thought are often quoted today as a counter to Keynes's arguments.

He also observed that wages and other input prices were not downwardly flexible. Workers did not readily accept pay decreases, nor did employers offer them. As a result, periods of high unemployment could persist as market forces did not function to bring the economy to full employment. The implication of these observations was that government intervention was necessary in the case of high unemployment.

KEYNES AND RECESSION

Given a recession, the Keynesian response is to increase government spending and to reduce income taxes in order to spur aggregate demand and return the economy to full employment. This means that government must be willing to run deficits in order to carry out the policy. On the bright side, Keynes shows that returning the economy to full employment can be done relatively cheaply because of the multiplier effect. If real GDP is $14 trillion but potential real GDP is $15 trillion, government does not have to spend $1 trillion to close the recessionary gap, but instead only a fraction of that because of the multiplier effect.

Here is how Keynes defined the multiplier effect. Keynes observed that individuals have a marginal propensity to consume and save. In other words, if you give people a dollar, they are inclined to spend some of it and save some of it. If government spent money on public works, the contractors and employees would then turn around and spend a portion of the resulting income and save the rest. This process would continue and lead to a multiplier effect throughout the economy.

For example, if Americans have a marginal propensity to consume 80% of their income, then an increase in government spending on infrastructure of $50 billion will result in $50 billion in government spending and then $40 billion of new consumer spending, followed by $32 billion and so on until eventually total spending equals $250 billion. How did that work? The $50 billion in government spending kicks off a continuing cycle of consumption and income. The higher the marginal propensity to consume, the higher the multiplier effect. Keynes also recognized that government spending yielded a larger multiplier effect than equal-sized tax cuts because people save a portion of their incomes. Thus, not all of the tax cuts' value is spent on consumption.

Keynes's observations and influence completely changed the study of economics. Today's policy framework is based on the ideas of Keynes and his followers. Although much of the modern debate is framed in terms of free-market capitalism versus socialism, Keynes was an advocate of capitalism, and his approach is better characterized as a hybrid form of capitalism than socialism.

THE INFLATION-UNEMPLOYMENT TRADE-OFF

The influence of Keynesian thought grew from the 1930s until the 1970s. The research of New Zealand–born economist A.W. Phillips helped reinforce Keynes's influence on governments during this period. Phillips studied the relationship between wage inflation and the unemployment rate in Britain and concluded that periods of wage inflation were associated with periods of low unemployment. Periods of stagnating wages were associated with periods of high unemployment. American economists Paul Samuelson and Robert Solow adapted the Phillips curve for the US economy. Using this model, they compared general price inflation (instead of wage inflation) to the unemployment rate. Many policymakers and economists reached the logical conclusion that Keynesian-style fiscal policies that stimulate AD could be used to sustain low unemployment at the cost of some known amount of inflation. The idea worked something like this: If policymakers wanted to reduce unemployment from 7% to 5%, the trade-off would be a known change in the inflation rate from 1% to 2%.

The experience of the 1970s caused some serious doubts about the legitimacy of the Phillips curve. Remember stagflation? During the 1970s, both inflation and unemployment simultaneously increased. These results did not align with the predictions of the Phillips curve, which implied the two were trade-offs.

Milton Friedman and Edmund Phelps viewed this real-world data as a disproof of the Phillips curve, and more importantly, of the validity of Keynesian economics. Friedman and Phelps introduced the natural rate hypothesis, which concluded that the rate of unemployment is independent of inflation in the long run. Efforts by government to reduce unemployment by creating temporary inflation would be ineffective. Workers would try to keep their real wages from falling by demanding higher nominal wages in line with inflation.

The Money Illusion

An assumption of Keynesian economics is that people suffer from money illusion. They prefer earning $100 per hour and paying $10 per gallon of gasoline to earning $10 per hour and paying $1 per gallon of gasoline. Even though real purchasing power is the same in each example, people have a strong preference for higher nominal wages.

The new consensus on the Phillips curve is that there are two types of curves. There is a short-run Phillips curve that implies a trade-off between inflation and unemployment, and there is a long-run Phillips curve that exists at an economy's natural rate of unemployment. Sampling a few years of inflation and unemployment data may suggest an inverse relationship between the two, but including all available data reveals no relationship between the two variables.

Economists chalk up changes in the short-run Phillips curve versus the long-run Phillips curve as being the result of changing inflation expectations. Phillips's original observations about the British economy were about a time period where expected inflation was stable. The breakdown of the adjustable peg exchange rate system in 1971 effectively ended any type of gold standard and introduced a period of uncertainty about inflation. The resulting increases in inflation expectations help to explain the increased inflation and unemployment that occurred. Short-run Phillips curves exist during periods of stable inflation expectations. When inflation expectations change, the short-run Phillips curve relationship breaks down, and either simultaneous increases or decreases in inflation and unemployment can occur. Once a new expected inflation rate embeds itself into the economy, a new short-run Phillips curve emerges.

Alan Greenspan attributes the reduction in inflation expectations as the reason for the low inflation and unemployment that occurred during his leadership as chair at the Fed. According to Greenspan, productivity gains from globalization subdued inflation fears for much of his tenure. Considering the influence of inflationary expectations, Keynesian policies will only work as long as inflation expectations remain stable. If the Keynesian AD policies create higher inflation expectations, they will be thwarted as attempts to stimulate AD and reduce unemployment will only create more inflation.

THE FEDERAL RESERVE SYSTEM

The Bank We Love to Hate

America has a long and storied love-hate relationship with its banking system. The most vilified institution is the nation's central bank—the Federal Reserve, or just the Fed. The Fed is not America's first central bank or even its second. Regardless of your feelings toward it or the history behind it, the Fed is at the center of the American economy and deserves your careful consideration.

HISTORY OF BANKING REVISITED

At the end of the American Revolution, the United States was saddled with significant war debt. In order to handle the debt and to create a unified currency, Alexander Hamilton proposed the creation of a central bank for the young nation. The First Bank of the United States, headquartered in Philadelphia, was modeled after the Bank of England. It served as the nation's central bank from its charter in 1791 until 1811 when the charter was allowed to expire.

In the nineteenth century, America went through a series of economic panics that led to the creation of another central bank. This bank eventually became a political target and failed to bring economic stability to the country.

The Second Bank of the United States was given a twenty-year charter in 1816 to help the US economy recover from the economic effects of the War of 1812. The Second Bank established a uniform currency and acted as a depository for the Treasury's accounts. The Second Bank of the United States was believed by many to be corrupt, and political pressure from President Jackson sealed its fate. In 1833, three years before its charter expired, Jackson had his Treasury secretary withdraw the US government's deposits from the bank and place them in state-chartered banks. This effectively killed the bank, and by 1841 the Second Bank of the United States was bankrupt.

During and after the Civil War, the United States created more national banks and reintroduced a single uniform currency. These national banks were instrumental in allowing the government to borrow by issuing bonds. Unlike the First and Second Banks of the United States, however, these national banks were decentralized.

The Bank Panic of 1907 was the impetus for creating the Federal Reserve System. A failed attempt by a Montana investor to corner the copper market led to a loss of confidence in the financial institutions associated with him and his brother. The contagion spread to unassociated institutions and, within a few days, an all-out run on the New York financial system was under way. Fortunately, J.P. Morgan and President Theodore Roosevelt's Treasury secretary brought calm to the situation by injecting cash into the banking system and eventually bringing an end to the bank runs. The Panic of 1907 showed that America needed a central bank to act as a lender of last resort to ensure liquidity in the banking system.

THE CREATION OF THE FEDERAL RESERVE SYSTEM

The 1913 passage of the Federal Reserve Act, signed into law by President Wilson, created the Federal Reserve System. Unlike previous attempts at central banking, the Fed drew from the strengths of its predecessors. Instead of creating a single central bank, the Federal Reserve Act established a decentralized, public-private banking system. The Fed is not headquartered in a single location, but has separate locations across the United States. The Federal Reserve is neither a purely governmental institution, nor is it a purely private institution. The Fed has features of both.

The Fed is the bank for the US government. The Treasury keeps its accounts with the US government and the government in turn writes checks from its accounts with the Fed. The taxes collected and the money borrowed through issuing government bonds are all deposited in the US Treasury's account with the Fed. Every time a taxpayer receives a refund, or a Social Security recipient receives their check, the checks are being drawn from the Treasury's account with the Fed.

Cash On Hand

Most of the money on deposit with the Federal Reserve exists in electronic form, but each of the district banks has a significant vault with millions of dollars under heavy security.

The Federal Reserve System's government arm, the Board of Governors, is headquartered in Washington, DC. The governors are appointed by the president of the United States and confirmed by the Senate for single, staggered fourteen-year terms. The Board is supervised by the chair and vice chair, who are also members of the Board. These two roles are appointed by the president and confirmed by the Senate for unlimited four-year terms. The Fed chair is the face of the

Federal Reserve System and is considered by many to be second in power only to the president of the United States when it comes to economic influence. The Board of Governors creates policy and regulations for the nation's banking system, sets reserve requirements, and approves changes in the discount rate. Since it returned to raising rates in March 2022, the Fed has changed the discount rate eleven times, bringing the fed funds rate to a twenty-two-year high of 5.50%. The strategy is being used to tame inflation and increase the cost of borrowing in the American economy.

In keeping with the United States' federal nature, the Fed is divided into twelve distinct geographic districts with headquarters for each district located in cities across the United States. Each district is an equal part of the Federal Reserve System. The district banks act as the bankers' banks and accept deposits from member banks. The district banks also perform a regulatory role in their district by monitoring the member banks and enforcing regulations within their respective districts. The district banks play a vital role in processing paper checks and electronic payments for the banking system. Finally, the district banks issue the currency to the banking system that they acquire from the US Department of the Treasury.

THE FOMC

The Federal Open Market Committee (FOMC) is the chief architect of the nation's monetary policy. The twelve voting members of the committee are made up of the Fed chair, the Board of Governors, the Federal Reserve Bank of New York's president, and four other district bank presidents who serve on a rotating basis, although all the district bank presidents are present at the committee meetings.

The FOMC meets eight times a year, or about once every six weeks, to review economic performance and decide the course of monetary policy by targeting the fed funds rate. FOMC meetings are closely monitored by the press and financial markets. Members of the media and investors carefully analyze the FOMC's press releases, looking for clues as to what might be the future direction of policy.

Briefcase Speculation

Investors attempting to profit by speculating on the Fed's interest rate policies would study the size of Alan Greenspan's briefcase during his tenure as Fed chair. They theorized that if the briefcase was big and heavy, he was carrying documentation to support his argument for changing interest rates. If the briefcase was light, then interest rates would probably remain unchanged.

US AND GLOBAL ECONOMIC INSTITUTIONS

Money Movers and Shakers

Whether they're government agencies, independent organizations, or private foundations, economic institutions keep trade moving and money flowing. Both American and global institutions play key roles in the respective economies, facilitating growth and development in an ever-changing economic landscape.

IRS

The Internal Revenue Service (IRS) strikes fear into the hearts of most Americans. But this essential agency plays a key role in the US economy. They oversee approximately 40 to 50% of the government's incoming cash flow in the form of individual income taxes annually, a critical part of the country's revenue. The IRS supports the economy by interpreting, administering, and enforcing the Internal Revenue Code, the country's income tax law. Contrary to popular belief the IRS does not create tax law; it merely executes tax law created by Congress. The agency also oversees management of gift, estate, and excise taxes.

The agency got its start as the Commissioner of Internal Revenue back in 1862 when President Lincoln needed money to fund the Civil War and created the first income tax. From there, it got renamed a few times and finally became the IRS in 1953.

In March 2020, in response to the ongoing COVID-19 crisis, the IRS was called upon to deliver Economic Impact Payments (EIPS, also called stimulus payments) to the American people. In all, there would be three rounds of EIPs, all administered by the IRS in an attempt to get funds to citizens as quickly as possible for an economic jumpstart.

Politicians often use tax increases or tax cuts to drive economic changes, counting on the IRS to make the new rules work. The tax code had been relatively steady since 2001 until the major overhaul of the Tax Cuts and Jobs Act of 2017. Since that, there have been several changes to tax policy, many related to the pandemic and its aftermath, with more proposed changes in the works. In the 2023 tax filing season alone, the IRS processed more than 161 million returns, collected $4.44 trillion in revenues, and issued more than 104 million refunds for a total of $320 billion.

Taking Down Criminals

Undercover IRS agents took down infamous gangster Al Capone in 1931. The elusive criminal ran an underground empire in Chicago, played a role in dozens of crimes including bootlegging, drug trafficking, robbery, and murder. But it was the IRS that caught him, and Capone was finally convicted for tax evasion.

US TREASURY

The US Department of the Treasury has its roots in the Revolutionary War. In September 1789, Congress created the Treasury, which would be led by Alexander Hamilton—its first secretary. As his first official act, Hamilton reported on the financial state of the country and suggested the first revenue source, a customs duty, to fund the nation's operations.

Over the years, the Treasury has been tasked with critical functions that included:

- Administering the Coast Guard (until 1967)
- Managing the Bureau of Narcotics (now part of the Justice Department)
- Creating and maintaining the federal budget (now performed by Office of Management and Budget)

Today, the Treasury continues to manage federal finances and directly impacts the state of the economy. It issues US government securities including Treasury bills, notes, and bonds—one of its most important functions that keeps the US economy running. Issuing and selling these securities help pay for the expenses that exceed government revenues, essentially using debt to fund the deficit. Interest rates on these securities affect interest rates on other borrowing, especially mortgages. The department also produces coins and paper money, supervises banks, offers advice on national and international economic policies, and enforces federal tax and financial laws.

WORLD BANK

Despite its name, the World Bank isn't technically a bank, though it does offer financial assistance to countries in need. Its focus is big picture, long-term economic development, with a goal of reducing poverty around the world. The World Bank supports developing countries by offering:

- Low-interest loans
- Grants
- Low- or no-interest credits

It encourages economic investment in areas like infrastructure, agriculture, education, public health, and natural resource management.

The World Bank was created in 1944 as part of the Bretton Woods Agreement. Over the decades, it's transformed into a group of five cooperative institutions now known as the World Bank Group. That includes the International Development Association, the International Bank for Reconstruction and Development, and the International Finance Corporation. Each organization plays a part to serve the World Bank's primary missions of helping advance developing nations and combating poverty through advice, funding, and research.

INTERNATIONAL MONETARY FUND

The International Monetary Fund, or IMF, offers financial assistance and guidance to member nations. The organization was created in 1944 along with the World Bank to help stabilize the global economy following World War II. Its funding comes directly from its 190 member countries, each according to the size of its economy, in the form of quota subscriptions. The main purpose of the IMF is to support global economic stability, putting out financial "fires" that threaten the stability and facilitating monetary policy and free trade.

The fund helps maintain the international monetary system, a critical piece of global trade, by providing a clear system for foreign exchange transactions. Special Drawing Rights (SDR) is a sort of reserve account held by the IMF, comprised of five currencies:

- US dollar
- Euro
- Chinese yuan
- Japanese yen
- British pound

SDR units measure the value of the basket of currencies, but an SDR is not technically money. It's more an accounting unit used to help stabilize the fund and provide liquidity support to struggling nations. Each member country gets an allocated share of SDRs in the reserve. Member countries can trade their SDRs for the hard currencies of other IMF members as needed.

WORLD TRADE ORGANIZATION

The World Trade Organization, or WTO, does exactly what its name suggests: It oversees global trade. The WTO plays several key roles in international trade including establishing and enforcing trade rules, providing a forum for trade negotiations, settling disputes among member nations, and lending support to developing economies.

The WTO has 164 members (as of 2023), representing more than 98% of total world trade, with an additional 25 observer nations, which is the status for countries hoping to join. In order to become part of the organization, a country's trade and economic policies must meet WTO standards and adhere to WTO member-nation rules.

This organization was created in 1995, replacing the General Agreement on Tariffs and Trade (GATT) that had been in place since 1947 following the devastation of World War II. The WTO focuses on lowering trade barriers and boosting trade among its member nations. Historically, there's been a clash between free trade and national protectionism. Globalization boosts the overall world economy but can end up hurting local communities and overlooking human rights. The biggest WTO supporters include multinational corporations, which greatly benefit from expanded free trade and reduced trade disputes.

MONETARY POLICY

Leave the Driving to Us

The goal of monetary policy is to promote price stability, full employment, and economic growth. The Fed, a monopolist over the money supply, is in a unique position to influence AD in the economy. Fed policy affects excess reserves in the banking system, which directly influences the money supply—which, in turn, changes interest rates. These changes in interest rates lead to changes in AD via consumption, investment, and net exports. The resulting change in AD affects GDP, inflation, and unemployment.

HOW THE FEDERAL RESERVE AFFECTS THE ECONOMY

The Federal Reserve influences the economy by applying pressure to interest rates and talking to the public. In the case of economic growth, the Fed can warn against inflation by ever so slightly raising interest rates whenever the economy seems to be growing too quickly. During periods of inflation, the Fed can mash down on the interest rate brake pedal, give a stern warning to the driver, and bring the economy back under control.

In the case of recession, the most the Fed can do is let off the brake pedal, or lower interest rates and encourage the driver to hit the gas. The Fed's power is asymmetrical; it is capable of stopping inflation, but only capable of encouraging full employment.

Reserve Requirement

A bank's reserve requirement is the percentage of checking account balances that the bank is not able to lend against. If the Fed were to raise the requirement, banks would have fewer excess reserves from which they could lend. This would reduce the money supply and result in higher interest rates, discouraging capital investment and durable goods consumption. This decrease in investment and consumption lowers AD and leads to less real GDP, higher unemployment, and a reduction in inflation. Lowering the reserve requirement would have the exact opposite effect.

Drawbacks to Changing the Reserve Requirement

The problem with changing the reserve requirement is that it is easy to lower, but much more difficult to raise. If the Fed lowers it, banks are able to lend more of their reserves and no real problem is created. However, raising the reserve requirement during periods of inflation would be nearly impossible for banks, as they probably have no excess reserves not already lent. The increase in the reserve requirement would precipitate an immediate liquidity crisis in the banking sector. Banks would call in loans and do whatever they could to meet the new higher requirement.

Discount Rate

The discount rate is the interest rate that member banks pay the Fed to borrow money overnight, usually when they are in financial distress. Raising the discount rate discourages borrowing, but lowering the discount rate encourages it. If the Fed wants to reduce inflation, it raises the discount rate. When the Fed does this, the following chain of events is set into motion: The Fed announces an increase in the discount rate; banks are discouraged from borrowing; excess reserves are less likely to be lent; the money supply does not grow; interest rates rise; consumption, investment, and net exports fall; AD decreases; GDP falls; unemployment rises; and inflation falls. Lowering the discount rate would have the exact opposite effect.

Drawbacks to Changing the Discount Rate

The problem with the discount rate is that banks are reluctant to borrow directly from the Fed. The reluctance stems from the fact that other forms of borrowing are available at lower rates, so going to the Fed's discount window is a public admission that something is wrong with the borrowing bank. A bank in good financial position will usually borrow to cover its short-term needs in the interbank lending market. The principal decision-makers at a bank do not want to scare away investors or current shareholders by borrowing from the Fed.

The discount rate is useful as a signal of future interest rate policy. This signaling function is important, as financial markets do not like surprises.

Open Market Operations

The primary way that the Fed enacts monetary policy is through the process known as open market operations (OMO). OMO is the buying and selling of US Treasury securities (Treasuries) between the Federal Reserve Bank of New York's open market desk and a select group of twenty-five primary security dealers. The dealers include most of the world's major banks and securities broker-dealers. They are expected to participate as counterparties to the Fed's open market operations and share market information with the Fed. OMO transactions have the effect of either increasing excess reserves in the banking system when the Fed buys Treasuries from the primary security dealers, or reducing excess reserves in the banking system when the Fed sells Treasuries to the primary dealers.

WHEN POLICIES COLLIDE: FISCAL/MONETARY MIXER

Federal Reserve policy does not exist in a political vacuum. Instead, monetary policy functions alongside government's fiscal policies. At times the two are at odds, but most of the time monetary policy is used to accommodate fiscal policy. For this to work, the Fed chair, the president, the Treasury secretary, and key members of Congress communicate to create a coherent policy that addresses the fundamental goals of price stability, full employment, and economic growth.

Money Talks

fiscal policy
The use of the federal budget in order to reduce unemployment or stabilize prices.

During periods of recession, expansionary fiscal policy is reinforced with expansionary monetary policy. When government spending increases and taxes decrease as part of expansionary fiscal policy, interest rates can rise. Expansionary monetary policy then offsets this pressure on interest rates by expanding the money supply and actively lowering short-term interest rates.

Inflationary periods are more problematic for presidents and lawmakers. The contractionary fiscal policy prescription calls for reduced spending and increased taxes, which are politically unpopular. Contractionary monetary policy is effective at stopping inflation, and the Fed's insulation from political pressure makes it perfectly suited for the task. Former Fed chair Paul Volcker was credited with whipping inflation when government was unable to do so.

MONETARY POLICY IN THE SHORT RUN AND THE LONG RUN

Monetary policy has different effects in the short run and the long run. Expansionary monetary policies designed to reduce short-term interest rates and spur full employment and economic growth eventually lead to higher interest rates as they induce inflation. This means that monetary policy must be carefully applied. If the Fed introduces a monetary stimulus, they must also plan to remove the stimulus in order to prevent future inflation. The problem for policymakers is in timing the policy. Early removal of the monetary stimulus might result in a protracted recession, but maintaining low interest rates for too long will almost certainly lead to higher inflation.

Too much reliance on monetary policy to reduce inflation can also lead to problems. Over the business cycle, if government uses expansionary fiscal policy to offset recessions and then relies on the Fed to contain periods of inflation, interest rates will ratchet up and long-term economic growth will be stymied. At some point government must rein in its spending and/or raise taxes to keep long-term interest rates from rising too high.

SUPPLY-SIDE ECONOMICS

The Rise of Voodoo Economics

The concurrent high unemployment and inflation of the 1970s was a painful period in American economic history. Stagflation came as a shock to many politicians and economists alike. By the 1970s, Keynesian economic thought was embedded in the minds of most policymakers. Although Milton Friedman and Edmund Phelps had publicly refuted the idea that there is stable trade-off between inflation and unemployment, policymakers were not quite willing to let go of the belief.

The Misery Index

Arthur Okun developed a simple index of economic hardship called the misery index. The misery Index is the sum of the unemployment rate and the inflation rate. Given normal conditions, the misery index is usually around 7%. During the Carter administration, the misery Index steadily increased because of stagflation and reached an all-time high of 21.98%.

The Keynesian economic framework so permeated policy decisions by the 1970s that data challenging the effectiveness of Keynesian economics created cognitive dissonance for many. When unemployment is high, government should spend more, and when inflation becomes a problem, the Fed should tighten spending. What stagflation presented was an intractable problem for many in positions of power. Spending to alleviate unemployment would only make inflation worse. Fed tightening spending would reduce employment. The policy options of those influenced by Keynes focused on either increasing or decreasing aggregate demand (AD). What to do? The answer offered by some was to focus on the supply side of the aggregate supply and aggregate demand model.

SUPPLY-SIDE ECONOMICS

Stagflation was fundamentally a supply problem, which is why a demand-side solution would not work. Classical economics' laissez-faire approach enjoyed something of a renaissance after Ronald Reagan's election. In the classical view of the economy, flexible and efficient markets ensure that the economy will maintain full employment. When recessions or periods of inflation set in, flexible input prices cause aggregate supply to increase or decrease and bring the economy back to full employment without government intervention. From the 1930s to the 1970s, there was a decrease in the flexibility and efficiency of the labor market. The supply-side argument was that government had gummed up the works and the markets needed to be de-Keynesed.

Deregulation, which began under President Carter, picked up steam under President Reagan. The airlines, which in the past had been heavily regulated by government, were set free and forced to compete with each other. This resulted in far more flights at cheaper prices. It also meant that the least efficient airlines were driven out of business.

Labor unions saw a decline in power under the Reagan administration. Foreign competition in the steel and car industries weakened the position of the unions. Probably the most powerful symbol of the loss in union power came at the hands of the newly elected president. The air traffic controllers union had lobbied for better pay and working conditions. In 1981, the union went on strike in violation of federal law. After being warned to return to work or be fired, over 11,000 air traffic controllers refused to return and were summarily fired by President Reagan. The message was clear.

While running for office, Reagan promoted the idea that tax cuts on high-income earners would enrich all Americans, as people had more incentive to spend and save. The spending and saving would lead not only to more consumption, but also more capital investment. As investment increases, businesses expand their productive capacity, and this leads to higher employment. The resulting increase in capital also leads to greater productivity, and eventually, lower prices.

The power of tax cuts to stimulate AD was well known to Keynesian economists. But the supply-side spin was that tax cuts would not only stimulate AD, but supply as well. At the same time that Reagan was proposing tax cuts, he also called for an increase in defense spending to counter the Soviet threat. Economists, politicians, and average people questioned the idea of simultaneously cutting taxes and increasing government spending. It appeared obvious that such a combination of policies would result in the federal government running large deficits as it spent more and taxed less.

CHALLENGES TO SUPPLY-SIDE ECONOMICS

Sometimes reality has a way of ruining a great idea. Reagan got his tax cuts and he got his increases in defense spending, but he also got huge deficits. Increased tax revenues failed to materialize. Instead, tax revenues drastically fell, and government budget deficits increased steadily during Reagan's administration.

A criticism of supply-side economics is that it effectively redistributes income to the rich. Because the mantra of supply-side economics is "tax cuts on income and capital gains," it stands to reason that the immediate beneficiary is going to be those with significant income.

Although supply-side economics is not mentioned much anymore, its arguments and logic are still part of the Republican and Libertarian political platforms. Cutting taxes, creating incentives for people to save and invest, and a general distrust of government involvement in the economy are supply-side ideas that still resonate with many voters. Democrats tend to promote a more populist agenda. Tax cuts for the middle class with tax increases on the wealthy, increased regulation of business, and the use of transfer payments to redistribute income are all ideas advanced by the Democrats and associated for good or bad with the Keynesians.

A COMPLETE TOOLBOX

Although supply-side economics as a field of study is frequently debated by mainstream economists, it has served to remind people that incentives matter. Policymakers must consider not only what voters want, but also how their policies shape the incentives of consumers and producers. Whenever government creates a new mandate that seeks to regulate economic behavior, it must also be prepared to deal with the unintended consequences that occur as the new mandate alters the incentives of individuals and institutions.

Ignoring the supply side of the economy leads to a unilateral approach to policymaking that ultimately boxes government into two choices: increase AD or decrease AD. By recognizing the role of aggregate supply, policymakers can promote more policy solutions to achieve their ultimate economic goals. For example, recognizing that a tax cut on personal income has demand-side and supply-side effects allows policymakers to sell the option to their diverse constituencies.

ECONOMIC GROWTH

Building a Better Society

In Jared Diamond's study of human history, *Guns, Germs, and Steel*, he talks about the question that prompted him to study the course of human events. As an avid bird watcher, Diamond took many trips to New Guinea, where he befriended a man named Yali. Yali asked Diamond why it was that the European descendants had so much while the people of New Guinea had so little. Diamond's fascinating account of the forces that shaped human history and the distribution of wealth is great reading. But for an economist, economic growth is described more simply—it's merely an increase in the GDP.

WHAT GROWTH MEANS

Economic growth occurs when there is a sustained increase in a nation's real GDP per person over time. Since 2000, the United States' real GDP has seen annual growth ranging from –3.4% to 5.7%, with an average rate of approximately 2%. This rate of growth means that the economy doubles in size about every thirty-six years. At the same time, the population increases at a rate of less than 1%, which means that current real GDP per capita is more than three times greater than in 1960. Economic growth is not guaranteed. Indeed, there are years in which no or negative growth occurs. These periods are associated with recession.

Growth reveals itself in positive and negative ways. Economic growth leads to increases in living standards, nutrition, healthcare, longevity, and material abundance. The downside is that economic growth often results in environmental destruction and increased income inequality. Economic growth as a goal for society is hotly debated, and both sides offer well-reasoned rationales for their positions.

WHY GROW?

Proponents of economic growth focus on the benefits it creates for society. The advances in food production, healthcare, longevity, and material abundance would not be possible without economic growth. Back in the late 1800s, most Americans were involved in agricultural production and subsisted on far fewer calories than today's Americans, less than 2% of whom are farmers. The average life span has increased from 39.4 in 1890 to 76.4 in 2023 because of the eradication of many diseases and advances in basic sanitation and healthcare. The quality and quantity of material goods has increased as well, allowing more Americans the things that only the wealthy could acquire in previous generations. The average workweek has decreased in the same period of time, allowing people more leisure. For most, economic growth has been a blessing.

Money and Happiness

Can money actually buy happiness? When economists compare GDP per capita with a country's overall level of happiness, an interesting trend occurs. As GDP per capita increases from $0 to $30,000, the level of happiness increases. This relationship seems to break down after that. So, to answer the question, the first $30,000 does buy happiness. After that, who knows?

As the economy grows and diversifies, more and more people are able to escape subsistence farming and pursue other areas of interest. This freedom to pursue education and vocations outside of farming did not exist for most of recorded history. The creative explosion of production that has occurred over the last 150 years has yielded advances in all fields of human endeavor. Where life was nasty, brutal, and short for most, it is now relatively humane, peaceful, and long. If you have ever visited an old cemetery, you might have noticed the number of graves for young children. What was once a common occurrence is now a rare tragedy. The diseases that ravaged the US population less than a century ago are for the most part eradicated. All of this is possible because of economic growth.

As people have become more specialized and more productive, their value to society has increased as well. Consider the amount of time and resources now devoted to raising an American child. The average American child has over $250,000 invested in their human capital. Aid organizations understand that increasing an individual's value to society is important for developing a stable, productive society.

CONDITIONS FOR ECONOMIC GROWTH

Planting the Seeds of Production

Economic growth doesn't happen by itself. It requires a number of different elements to occur. Some of these elements are obvious; for example, people and resources are both needed to make products. But others are less obvious. Consider countries where laws are not equitably enforced. Can sustainable economic growth occur?

HUMAN CAPITAL

The most important element in economic growth is human capital. Human capital consists of the education, skills, and abilities possessed by an individual. Countries that invest heavily in human capital tend to have more economic growth than similarly endowed countries that do not. The United States is one of the world leaders in developing human capital. Compulsory primary and secondary education, mandatory vaccinations, and abundant nutrition have contributed to making America the sixth-most productive nation on earth. Few nations spend more on educating and developing human capital than the United States.

Individual freedom and the ability to acquire private property are also essential elements in developing human capital. When individuals are free to choose their vocation and enjoy the benefits of private property, their productivity is higher than in places where individual freedom or private property is not valued. By way of comparison, the average German was far more productive in capitalist West Germany than in communist East Germany, and the average South Korean today is far more productive than the average North Korean, because economic freedom provides the incentive to produce more in order to have more.

Population Growth and Economic Growth

To have human capital, you must have humans. For economies to develop and grow, it is important that the population grows as well. Population growth must also occur alongside productivity growth. Larger populations are capable of producing more output as well as more innovation because the greater the population, the greater the number of productive resources. The more people a country has, the more probable entrepreneurs it has. And entrepreneurs are one of the drivers of economic growth.

The presence of immense natural resources can sometimes be a deterrent to developing human capital. The paradox of natural resource wealth is that governments are often so eager to exploit their natural resources for export that they neglect to invest in their population's human capital. At first glance, a comparison of Russia and Japan would lead most observers to believe that Russia is far wealthier than Japan. After all, it has the largest deposits of minerals and other natural resource wealth in the world. Japan, on the other hand, has few natural resources. However, Japan has enjoyed much greater economic growth because it has invested far more in its human capital.

PHYSICAL CAPITAL

Developing human capital alone is not enough to create economic growth. Economies must also invest in developing physical capital. Physical capital is the tools, factories, and equipment that are used in the production process. As the stock of physical capital increases, the nation experiences capital deepening. Capital deepening refers to the amount of capital available to each worker. Capital deepening provides for a more productive labor force. The US has more than $69 trillion invested in physical capital. This is one of the reasons for America's productivity edge.

Because physical capital is the result of investment, interest rates play a key role in its development. Low, stable interest rates encourage investment. In the short run, investment creates increased AD, but in the long run it expands the economy's stock of capital. High interest rates or unstable interest rates are injurious to investment decisions and result in the formation of less capital.

Once capital is deployed, it must be maintained. Capital needs adequate infrastructure to realize its potential. Roads, waterways, rail systems, and reliable utility systems make capital easier to access and greatly improve the chances that it will be used effectively. One of the failures of the Soviet Union was an ineffective use of capital. The Soviets built factories that dwarfed their Western counterparts. But because of inadequate infrastructure, they were often difficult to get to. This made distributing their output more difficult. The developing world lacks steady sources of power and the transportation networks that are necessary for efficient use of factories. Europe, Japan, and the United States, by comparison, have ample infrastructure to facilitate the continuous use and transport of capital's output.

RESEARCH AND DEVELOPMENT

Creativity, innovation, and invention are necessary for economic growth to continue. Firms in industrialized nations such as the US and Japan spend far more on research and development compared to firms in the developing world. Research and development requires sacrificing current profits in order to gain even greater profits in the future. For firms to take this risk, incentives must exist and be protected. Patents, which provide legal protection for inventors, provide the protection firms need to realize the profits of their research and development.

If developing countries want to continue economic growth, they must find ways to encourage innovation. China's impressive growth over the last several years has mainly come from a shift from manufacturing to valuable services along with a shift from investment to consumption among its citizens. Although China has many capable, intelligent, and innovative people, the laws in China do not adequately protect intellectual property. Very little incentive exists for Chinese manufacturers to spend money on research and development of new products if the factory next door can just copy them and produce them without expending the research dollars. Over time, expect to see China make strides in protecting the intellectual property of its manufacturers.

THE RULE OF LAW

Another condition for growth is the rule of law. Government officials should obey the law and should also apply the law uniformly and fairly. Corruption and cronyism discourage domestic and foreign investment by effectively raising the cost of capital. Firms, individuals, and foreign investors must know that their property is protected by law. One reason that capital investment is lacking in the developing world stems from the fact that corrupt governments are far more likely to seize private property in the name of national interests. Venezuela's seizure of foreign-owned oil fields in 2007 most likely deters future foreign investment. Unlike Venezuela, former British colonies such as the United States, Canada, Australia, New Zealand, and Hong Kong inherited the English common law with its emphasis on private property, which makes them safe and attractive to foreign investors. Foreign owners of capital have basically the same rights as domestic investors. As a result, more capital accumulates in these countries compared to most others.

HOW ECONOMIC POLICY AFFECTS GROWTH

The Government Gets Involved

Government policies also play a role in determining economic growth. Stabilization policies by the central bank affect interest rates and thus capital investment. Fiscal policy impacts capital investment indirectly through the effect of government debt on interest rates. Tax policies that affect consumption and saving decisions influence economic growth by way of their impact on interest rates and work incentives.

INTEREST RATE POLICY

The Fed promotes economic growth when it maintains a predictable, stable interest rate policy. Although monetary policy primarily affects short-term interest rates, it is the Fed's effect on long-term interest rates that influences growth. Firms are unlikely to make long-term investments in capital if they are uncertain about future interest rates and inflation. To avoid uncertainty, the Fed must maintain a firm lid on actual and expected inflation. The Fed's policy stance during a recession is to target a lower fed funds rate to encourage borrowing. However, if the Fed keeps interest rates too low for too long, future inflation is more likely. This expected inflation and increased long-term interest rates will discourage capital investment and, ultimately, long-run economic growth. Short-term increases in interest rates to dampen inflation may not please Wall Street, but since the increases reduce expected inflation, they help to keep long-term interest rates low and stable. And low, stable long-term interest rates encourage capital investment.

Fiscal policy that does not lead to a balanced budget impacts long-term interest rates and capital investment. Budget deficits in the absence of capital inflow or increased domestic saving lead to higher long-term interest rates and hinder investment in capital. If capital inflows or domestic savings are enough to offset government borrowing, the interest rate effect of a deficit is negated. Regardless of immediate interest rate effects, budget deficits, if large enough, create uncertainty and may effectively discourage investment. The presence of budget surpluses reduces long-term interest rates and encourages capital investment.

TAX POLICY

Changes in tax policy affect businesses and are likely to also impact the rate of economic growth. Increasing the tax burden on firms reduces their ability and incentive to invest in capital. Increasing the capital gains tax on financial investors reduces the flow of savings firms use to make real investments in physical capital. Businesses faced with too high a tax burden may choose to produce elsewhere. It is important to understand that capital is free to flow. Placing taxes on businesses, although politically popular, is a recipe for reduced growth.

Taxes on personal income affect work incentives and can thus also influence the rate of growth. In the United States, the more productive you are, the more income you earn. The more income you earn, the higher your marginal tax rate. This is what economists call a progressive tax system. If tax rates are increased on upper incomes, they increase the tax burden of the most productive members of society. Although American tax rates are much lower than in Europe, given a high enough tax rate, the productive worker will either reduce productivity or move to where productivity is not taxed as highly. So far, America has been the beneficiary of high tax rates in Europe. Europe has suffered a brain drain as its best and brightest (those who are highly taxed) move toward countries with lower tax rates.

Money Talks

flat tax

A flat tax is one that taxes all households at the same rate regardless of the level of income. Given a flat tax of 15%, a household earning $40,000 would pay $6,000 in taxes, while a household earning $100,000 would pay $15,000 in taxes. The benefit of a flat tax is its simplicity. The downside is that for many households, a flat tax would represent an increase in their tax burden. Even though many are in the 22% to 35% marginal tax brackets, their average tax rates are much lower because of exemptions, deductions, and the fact that the marginal tax rate is only on the incremental income and not the total income.

The brain drain is serious enough that European countries are establishing programs to encourage expatriates to migrate back and to welcome new residents (maybe they should try a tax cut). Europe's loss is America's gain as human capital has increased steadily in the United States.

THE DOWNSIDES TO
ECONOMIC GROWTH

Economic growth is not without its downsides or its detractors. Economic growth has led to increased income inequality, which, if ignored, threatens continued economic growth. Over the last fifty years, income inequality in the United States has increased for a variety of reasons. The loss of union power, reduction in marginal tax rates, foreign competition, and meritocracy are some frequently cited reasons. Union membership has steadily declined since the 1980s, and as a result, workers have lost leverage in negotiating wages. This decline has occurred because of structural changes in the economy and as a result of government taking a more adversarial role with unions. Decreases in marginal tax rates have also widened the gap between low- and high-income earners.

According to the Census Bureau, from 1980 to 2008, the bottom quintile of households saw little or no change in average household income, while the top saw a steady increase in income. Globalization has contributed to income inequality. Much of this country's unskilled manufacturing has moved overseas, leaving unskilled Americans in lower-paying service-sector jobs. Another theory of why income inequality has increased has to do with the development of a meritocracy. In a meritocracy, the best and brightest marry the best and brightest and reproduce more of the best and brightest, leaving the not so best and not so bright in the proverbial dust.

For economic growth to continue, the gains must be more evenly distributed across the population. Whether that is fair or not is irrelevant. America practices both capitalism and democracy. The more productive members of society are rewarded by capitalism, while less-productive or less-skilled members of society see their income stagnate. This fact does not sit well with the latter and creates an opportunity for a political solution. Though not all Americans see the direct benefits of capitalism, they do have a vote. Therefore, those who wind up on the short end of capitalism's stick are likely to exercise their right to vote and change the equation. Income redistribution is a fact of life in a society with universal suffrage. Proponents of economic growth must be prepared to share their earned gains with those who may not have earned it.

THE GREAT DEPRESSION MEETS THE GREAT RECESSION

History Repeats Itself, Sort Of

Before 2007, had you ever heard of subprime mortgages, CDOs, or credit default swaps? In 2007, one of the worst financial crises in US history began. Through 2008 and 2009 the financial crisis became a global recession. The scale of the financial and economic crisis is measured in tens of trillions of dollars.

LINKS TO THE GREAT DEPRESSION

Of course you can't talk about the Great Recession without talking first about the Great Depression, another economic disaster that affected the country for years. You may recall that stock prices began to drop in the fall of 1929 and then crashed on October 29 of that year, a day known as Black Tuesday. Over the next ten years, personal income plunged, investment stalled, unemployment reached a high of 25%, and international trade plummeted.

Unfortunately, the Fed, which was created after an earlier banking crisis (the Panic of 1907), was put to the test during the Great Depression, where it failed to provide the necessary liquidity to stem another systemic bank panic. Critics of the Fed place much of the blame for the severity of the Depression on the Fed. The general consensus is that the Fed restricted the flow of credit when it should have flooded the system with inexpensive credit.

After the stock market collapse in 1929 and the ensuing financial and economic crisis, Congress passed the Glass-Steagall Act of 1933, which created the Federal Deposit Insurance Corporation (FDIC) to insure bank deposits and prevent future bank runs. Glass-Steagall also prohibited commercial banks from engaging in most investment activities. Fast forward to 1956, when the Bank Holding Company Act was created to prohibit banks from underwriting insurance, further reinforcing provisions of Glass-Steagall. Bank regulations had the effect of restoring confidence in the industry. That confidence wouldn't last long, however.

THE RUN-UP TO THE MELTDOWN

The Great Recession, as it is often called, had its beginnings in the twentieth century during a period of deregulation and rampant financial innovation. The Depression-era Glass-Steagall Act, which acted as a barrier between commercial banks and investment banks, was repealed in 1999 and a new shadow banking industry was created. At the same time, the Fed and government regulators increasingly relied on business to regulate itself, believing that market forces would lead to self-enforcement of sound practices.

Expectations and Reality

Consumer and producer expectations are important forces in the economy. Positive expectations tend to boost economic activity while negative expectations tend to suppress economic activity. The president and the Fed chair are as much cheerleaders for economic optimism as they are serious policymakers.

The impact of the September 11, 2001 terrorist attacks created fear in a by-then retreating stock market. This fear helped to send the United States into a shallow recession in 2001. The Federal Reserve responded by immediately lowering the fed funds rate and injecting large amounts of money into the banking system.

These injections, along with the Bush tax cuts, two wars, and a deregulated financial sector, led to a pool of money that created a boom in residential and commercial real estate investment. Much of the spending that occurred during the years 2002 through 2005 was fueled by home-equity borrowing at historically low rates of interest. Deregulated banks added fuel to the fire by lending money to pretty much anybody who showed up for a loan. Consumers went on a credit spending binge as the booming housing market created a wealth effect.

In 2006, the overheated housing market began to slow down. Savvy investors soon began pulling away from housing and putting money into commodities like oil and precious metals. In 2007, the housing market went into complete free-fall while oil prices shot up. This combination of events brought the spending party to a halt as consumers saw their wealth decreasing at the same time highly visible energy and food prices increased. Real estate investors, and eventually homeowners, began to walk away from properties that were now worth less than the balance on the mortgages.

SECURITIZATION

One of the culprits in the run-up to the meltdown was a financial innovation called securitization. Traditionally, banks made loans to customers, carried the loan on their balance sheet, and earned profit from the interest and fees. This gave banks a strong incentive to carefully assess a borrower's risk of default. With shareholders hungry for ever-greater returns, banks felt pressured to increase profits by expanding their lending activities. Banks delivered these profits by becoming loan originators that charged fees to make the original loans, which they then sold to investment banks. The investment banks packaged the loans into bundles and sold them as a type of bond called a collateralized debt obligation (CDO).

CDOs were sold to institutional investors, insurance companies, other banks, and hedge funds. The investors believed that CDOs were a sound investment because borrowers usually pay their mortgages, and if they don't, the property is used as collateral. The popularity of CDOs expanded, which increased the size of the market, letting banks lend more as a ready market existed for their loans. Banks offered even lower interest rates and relaxed their underwriting standards, which led to more loans being offered and packaged as CDOs even while housing prices increased. This created a vicious cycle that would eventually come crashing down, and the economy took years to rebound. When it did, it flourished, until a global pandemic turned everything upside down.

FOLLOW-UP:
THE PANDEMIC RECESSION

Though it didn't last as long or fall as far as the Great Recession, the COVID-19 pandemic recession took a great toll on the American economy. This brief economic downturn had significant economic fallout as lockdowns, shuttered businesses, and supply chain issues changed life virtually overnight. The US government responded with stimulus payments, special forgivable business loans, and other monetary measures to keep the economy at least limping along. The Fed supported that by purchasing enormous quantities of Treasury securities. The COVID-19 recession technically lasted only two months in 2020, but its effects were felt for the next couple of years.

THE COLLAPSE OF INVESTMENT BANKING

Bursting a Bubble

Many of the institutional investors, banks, and pension funds have conservative investment policies that limit the types of investments they can make. These investors rely on bond rating agencies like Moody's and Standard & Poor's to determine the overall level of risk of an investment. Some can only invest in AAA or AA+ rated bonds, but many aren't limited in this way. AAA or AA+ bonds are the highest ratings and typically indicate that the investment is extremely safe. Many of the CDOs that investors bought had these high ratings.

RISK MANAGEMENT AND CREDIT DEFAULT SWAPS

The underlying problem was that the rating agencies were only rating the top layer of the CDO. The CDOs are divided into tranches, or parts, with secure, high-quality loans in the top tranche, and lesser-quality loans in the lower tranches. The CDOs were packaged this way so that they would yield higher returns to the investors. The lower, riskier tranches paid higher interest rates, which made the entire CDO have a higher yield than a CDO made up of only high-quality mortgages.

The Principal-Agent Problem Strikes Again

Once again, a principal-agent problem was at work. The rating agencies earn fees from those marketing the CDOs, so they have an incentive to award high ratings to their customers' products. In addition, many CDOs were structured in ways that worked around agency rules to garner higher ratings. The institutional investors are investing other people's money, so as long as they are following the protocol and buying the highly rated investment, they have little incentive to do anything other than maximize the return to their paying customers.

To sweeten the deal, some investment banks that marketed CDOs to investors sold a type of insurance called a credit default swap (CDS) that would pay the investor if the CDO went into default. For the investor, this was enough to make CDOs the perfect investment. For the investment banks, they were making money hand over fist selling the CDOs and then again charging for the CDSs. Profits went through the roof, as did the incentive for managers and chief executive officers to market these products to their customers. There was only one small problem. The CDOs were much less secure than people believed and the CDSs were not adequately funded. If the CDOs were to default en masse, the investment banks that sold the CDSs would be liable for hundreds of billions of dollars. That is exactly what happened.

THE CRISIS HITS
INVESTMENT BANKING

The investment bank Bear Stearns was the first Wall Street victim of the mortgage crisis. Bear Stearns had heavily marketed CDOs and also invested in them. In the face of heavy financial losses, Bear Stearns's balance sheet became toxic. Soon other investment banks refused to lend to Bear Stearns, and the company faced insolvency. The New York Federal Reserve president, Timothy Geithner, orchestrated a bailout of Bear Stearns by lending money to banking giant JPMorgan Chase to purchase Bear Stearns at a deep discount. It was hoped that this would prevent a widespread panic, but the opposite happened. Soon Lehman Brothers was on the ropes, but this time no one came to the rescue. The panic had spread.

Money Talks

moral hazard

A moral hazard is created when insurance or expectation of a government bailout encourages risk-taking behavior. Economists and policymakers must address moral hazard when making decisions. Failure to do so encourages more risk-taking. Ignoring moral hazard is a moral hazard.

As CDOs defaulted, investors exercised their CDSs, which insurance giant AIG had marketed. AIG faced losses of hundreds of billions of dollars, and that would have occurred without a federal assist. Many on Wall Street and in Washington, DC, believed that AIG was "too big to fail," so the government took the unprecedented action of bailing out AIG to prevent further catastrophe.

With the high-profile failure of two of America's largest investment banks and the bailout of AIG, financial institutions stopped
lending to each other and banks soon stopped lending altogether.
Business ground to a halt. The Great Recession had begun. Eventually, investment banks restabilized. But in 2023, tremors in the
industry resurfaced.

CREDIT SUISSE COLLAPSES

Credit Suisse was a key player among global investment banks.
Founded in 1856, it grew to become Switzerland's second largest
bank with more than $1.7 trillion of assets under management.
For 150 years, it stood as a shining example, but the bank became
plagued by scandal after scandal starting in 2019. By 2021, Credit
Suisse was in trouble and the pandemic economy led to nearly $1
billion in losses. When rumors of impending failure circulated, cli-
ents rushed to withdraw nearly $119 billion in 2022, its stock value
plummeted, and investors lost confidence. In March 2023, Credit
Suisse came up with a plan to borrow $54 billion, but that would not
transpire. That same month, Swiss authorities allowed UBS (the largest bank in Switzerland) to take over Credit Suisse. The fallout from
Credit Suisse's failure is ongoing as of November 2023, as thousands of employees face uncertain futures and as international faith
in Switzerland as the most stable banking system remains shaken.

FISCAL POLICY UNDER FIRE

You're Going to Need a Bigger Boat

The collapse of the mortgage security market in the Great Recession meant that trillions of dollars' worth of financial assets had become worthless. This economic recession was a deadly combination of a financial crisis compounded with a wider economic crisis. In the face of economic recession, the Keynesian prescription is for expansionary monetary and fiscal policy to stimulate the economy. The problem was that the tools of policy that are normally effective were both severely hampered.

THE FED

The usual prescription for a recession is for the Fed to buy Treasury bills from primary security dealers and then allow the money creation process to work its magic. When banks are unwilling to lend, this prescription does not work. Instead of money being created, the financial system was destroying money. Because many of the failures in the financial system had occurred outside of traditional banking, the Fed was hard-pressed to get money where it needed to be.

The Fed is set up by law to work with the banks. The tools it has at its disposal are aimed at banks, but this financial crisis was different. The shadow banking system that had been created by deregulation was out of the scope of the Fed. In order for the Fed to get things working again, the shadow system had to be transformed into the more regulated traditional banks. That is what they did. Goldman Sachs and Morgan Stanley, the last of the great investment banks, changed their status under SEC regulations and submitted to the Fed.

Quantitative Easing

The Fed began inventing new tools of monetary policy. The first was the Term Auction Facility (TAF), which allowed banks to bid on loans from the Fed without the downside risk of borrowing from the discount window. The Fed started buying up mortgage-backed securities and agency debt. Ultimately what the Fed was doing was creating markets for assets in exchange for cash, a process called quantitative easing.

Most of these tools expired by March 2010. The FOMC reduced its target for the fed funds rate to 0%. This is as expansionary as the Fed can get with open market operations.

Government Gets Inventive

The government also responded to the banking crisis by taking extraordinary measures. Congress and the president, first Bush and then Obama, planned a massive policy response. But the government was already engaged in heavy-duty fiscal expansion. Taxes were extremely low and spending was extremely high. Economists questioned how much more stimulus government could deliver.

Congress passed the Troubled Asset Relief Program (TARP) in 2000, giving the Treasury the ability to recapitalize the banks that had been hit hard by the collapse of the housing market and CDOs. This was only the beginning of the government's efforts to stabilize the economy. In 2009, the government also purchased control of failing automaker General Motors for $50 billion to keep it from going out of business.

To stimulate investment in housing, the government implemented a substantial $8,000 tax credit for homebuyers. Unemployment benefits were extended for millions of out-of-work Americans. With the American Recovery and Reinvestment Act of 2009, the government spent around $840 billion in order to expand the economy. Some economists believe that the government and central bank's response to the crisis averted a second Great Depression.

Theory versus Practice

Theories affect the way economists and policymakers tell the story of what is actually happening. These narratives of reality have the power to affect reality if enough people believe them. The story of expected inflation creating inflation is a powerful story, and if policymakers do not address it, the story could become the reality.

The Tax Cuts and Jobs Act

The 2017 Tax Cuts and Jobs Act (TCJA, also known as the Trump tax cuts) were met with skepticism by economists and glee by corporate America. The changes delivered permanent reductions in corporate tax rates and temporary tax benefits (set to expire in 2025) for individuals. The Congressional Budget Office projected these policies would balloon the deficit by an estimated $1.9 trillion over a ten-year period. The government hoped that that TCJA tax cuts would stimulate the economy with increased corporate investment.

Economists found that while corporate investment did increase, it was not nearly as much as projected. In addition, the tax cuts were implemented at the same time as changes in trade policy, making it difficult to specify where economic changes and growth were coming from. Economists were also concerned that the related deficit increases could have long-term negative effects on the economy at large, calling the TCJA a "deficit-funded tax cut."

COVID-19 Programs under Fire

The government created many supportive programs to ease the financial burdens of the COVID-19 pandemic. Many of those were heavily criticized as unwarranted giveaways, especially as around $742 billion in PPP (Paycheck Protection Program) loans were forgiven. It came to light that millionaires, billionaires, celebrities, and members of Congress had received PPP loans and had them forgiven. And with the rush to distribute funds, billions of dollars of relief funding were lost to fraud.

For many families and small businesses, COVID-19 programs brought much-needed relief that would disappear as the funding wound down. For example, as pandemic related support for childcare facilities ended, more than seventy thousand such facilities were set to close, leaving more than three million children without daycare spots. This could have long-reaching effects on the economy as some parents could be pushed out of the labor force without access to childcare.

THE ENVIRONMENT AND THE ECONOMY

Tree-Huggers Unite!

Most Americans believe that protecting the environment is a valuable goal for our society. The way that government and environmentalists have gone about achieving this goal has for the most part ignored the realities of economics. The Endangered Species Act, the Clean Air Act, and the Clean Water Act all have laudable goals. Critics of the legislation are not pro-extinction, pro-smog, and pro-dirty water. For most, the criticism is in how these goals are achieved and not the goals themselves. Economists offer a unique perspective on the environment, and inclusion of economic principles can be used to bring about the goal of environmental protection more efficiently and with greater utility.

IS GROWTH SUSTAINABLE?

One of the costs of an ever-growing economy is the strain that it places on the environment. As the population expands more and more, resources are required to sustain the population. This growth need not necessarily lead to environmental collapse. Instead, markets can be used to alter the incentives of individuals and firms as they face trade-offs in their use of resources.

Demand for resources tends to increase the price of those resources. As the price increases, individuals and firms that use these resources face an incentive to use less in the case of nonrenewables.

In the case of renewable resources, entrepreneurs gain an incentive to increase the production of the renewable resource. These incentives are powerful and efficient.

Renewable Resources

Consider the case of lumber, a renewable resource. Increased demand for lumber has led to an increase in the price of lumber. This price increase leads tree farmers to expand their output to meet the demand. The net effect of increased demand for lumber is increased demand for forests. Increased demand for forests makes the land more desirable and leads to more land being placed into forest production. Some would argue that if you cut down the trees, eventually there will be none left. However, this statement ignores economic incentives. Would there be more corn or less corn if people stopped eating it? If you answered less, you would be correct. If people stop eating corn, farmers have no incentive to grow corn. Likewise, if people eat more corn, then farmers grow more corn. The same is true with trees. Trees take longer to grow, though, and as a result they're priced much higher than corn.

Nonrenewable Resources

In the case of nonrenewables like coal, oil, and natural gas reserves, markets provide incentives to both producers and consumers. As demand increases for these factors of production, the price increases. This leads to higher prices and higher costs of production for firms that use the resources. These higher costs provide firms with an incentive to become more efficient in the use of the resource. For example, if a firm uses natural gas in production and gas prices rise, the firm has a strong incentive to use its natural gas in the most efficient way possible. Firms that are wasteful and inefficient will find it difficult to compete against firms that use resources more efficiently. They'll eventually go out of business.

Economic Efficiency

Economic efficiency occurs as resources are used with less waste. Efficiency should be a goal of not only economists, but anyone who cares about the planet. Less waste means that fewer resources are required in production.

The Role of Incentives

Protecting endangered species is important to many people. There is considerable political pressure for governments to enact legislation to protect species. One possible way to protect endangered species that is supported by economists is to promote them as food (meat to consume), though that only works with a limited number of species.

Why did the American bison population almost go extinct while the cow population increased exponentially? Is it because the cows ate the bison? No, one reason bison faced extinction while cows thrived is because cows were private property while bison were not. Political motivations, such as driving out Native American populations and paving the way for railroads, also played key parts. The population of bison fell from the millions to just over a thousand by 1889. Today, fortunately, the American bison is back from the brink of extinction because they became private property. Today there are more than 500,000 bison, and their numbers are growing as a market has developed for bison meat.

THE RIGHT TO POLLUTE

Pollution is an economic bad. All production processes create some form of pollution, so zero pollution is not a reasonable goal. The right amount, or socially optimal amount, of pollution occurs when the marginal social benefit equals the marginal social cost of production. That means that firms should produce to the point where the extra benefit of production to society equals the extra cost, inclusive of the cost of pollution to society. Firms do not pay the cost of pollution, and so they produce too much output and thus too much pollution. In order to get firms to produce the appropriate amount of pollution, the cost of pollution must enter into their production decision. Governments can tax or sell pollution permits. Another option is for affected individuals who bear the cost of pollution to negotiate a payment from the polluter.

Per-Unit Taxes

A per-unit tax on production could be used to reduce the amount of pollution that the firm produces. The tax on the producer increases the cost of production, which reduces their willingness and ability to produce their product. The result is less production, and therefore, less pollution. The problem with a per-unit tax is that it would likely be levied on all producers in an industry, so cleaner, more efficient producers are taxed at the same rate as heavier polluters. The tax reduces pollution in the industry, but does not increase the incentive for individual producers to clean up their act. Also, if demand for the good or service increases, then the quantity of pollution would still increase.

Cap and Trade

Government regulations designed to limit the total levels of certain industrial chemical emissions, especially carbon dioxide, are called cap and trade programs. They strive to reduce harm to the environment without doing harm to the economy. Though there are several ways these programs can work, they tend to follow a specific pattern:

- The government sets an emissions cap for an industry
- A set number of annual permits are issued, with each permit allowing a specific amount of pollutants
- The permits are either distributed or auctioned off
- Companies are taxed if they emit more pollutants than the permit allows
- The number of permits are reduced each year, which also reduces the overall emissions cap
- Companies can sell or trade their permits to other companies

Pollution Permits

Another option is to create a market for pollution permits, which fall under the cap and trade umbrella. A working example is permits called carbon credits (also called carbon offsets), which let producers of carbon dioxide purchase permission to create greenhouse gases. Each carbon credit allows one metric ton of carbon dioxide. Credits can be purchased or created by entities that reduce or remove carbon dioxide (for example, by installing solar panels or through reforestation). Countries and companies can buy or sell carbon credits on one of the dozens of carbon markets that exist worldwide. This scheme encourages firms to become more efficient and reduce pollution simultaneously. Unlike pollution taxes, this solution rewards firms for reducing pollution instead of punishing all firms equally.

Climate Exchanges

Climate exchanges exist worldwide for trading permits in various industrial pollutants. Climate exchanges act much like stock exchanges, allowing firms to buy and sell permits. In the future, students interested in the environment and economics may become climate brokers.

The Coase Theorem

A final option for firms that pollute or harm the environment is to directly pay those who are harmed by the pollution. This option is referred to as the Coase theorem. Ronald Coase, a British-born economist, suggested that an efficient outcome could be achieved if polluters and those who bear the cost directly negotiated a payment that was acceptable to both parties. Some assumptions of the Coase theorem are that there are no bargaining costs for either party, property rights are clearly defined, and the number of people involved is small.

The Nature Conservancy and Sierra Club use this strategy to preserve environmentally sensitive areas, buying up the land themselves. Many concerned with the environment have applied this strategy in preserving the rainforest. It is much easier to save a forest that you own than to save a forest that everyone owns. In the end, economic principles can be used to achieve environmental goals effectively and efficiently.

INDEX

ABOUT THE AUTHORS

Alfred Mill has a deep interest in personal finance and economics. He is the author of *Personal Finance 101*, *Economics 101*, and *Social Security 101*.

Michele Cagan is a CPA, author, and financial mentor. With more than twenty years of experience, she offers unique insighto into personal finances, from breaking out of debt and minimizing taxes to maximizing income and building wealth. Michele has written numerous articles and books about small business finances, investing, and accounting, including *The Infographic Guide to Personal Finance*, *Real Estate Investing 101*, *Investing 101*, *Budgeting 101*, and *The Financial Recovery Workbook*. In addition to her financial know-how, Michele has a not-so-secret love of painting, Star Wars, and chocolate. She lives in Maryland with her kid, dogs, cats, and koi. Get more financial guidance from Michele by visiting MicheleCaganCPA.com.

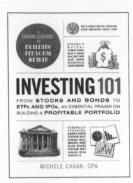